A Diamond

IN THE ROUGH

COWBOYING AROUND

A Diamond

IN THE ROUGH

LLOYD PERRY

TATE PUBLISHING & Enterprises

Published by Tate Publishing & Enterprises, LLC
127 E. Trade Center Terrace | Mustang, Oklahoma 73064 USA
1.888.361.9473 | www.tatepublishing.com

Tate Publishing is committed to excellence in the publishing industry. The company reflects the philosophy established by the founders, based on Psalm 68:11,
"The Lord gave the word and great was the company of those who published it."

Book design copyright © 2011 by Tate Publishing, LLC. All rights reserved.
Cover design by Shawn Collins
Interior design by Sarah Kirchen

Published in the United States of America

ISBN: 978-1-61346-092-4
1. Biography & Autobiography / Personal Memoirs
2. Religion / Christian Life / Personal Growth
11.07.28

DEDICATION

I dedicate this book to my mentor in Christ,
Mr. Clyde Copeland.

A diamond is a piece of coal that does well under pressure.

TABLE OF CONTENTS

FOREWORD

*I*n finding Lloyd Perry's *A Diamond in the Rough,* you have discovered a true jewel. In its pages you will find entertainment, information, and inspiration. You will hear about practical jokes that men of the range play on one another. You will learn some of the colorful vocabulary of raising cattle, training dogs, and hunting hogs. You will come to appreciate a cowboy's dedication to the unwritten code of the American West. Above all, you will appreciate the reverence of a Christian cowboy for his LORD and how that reverence is expressed in every phase of his life and work.

There are many adventures in *A Diamond in the Rough.* In between adventures, you will often hear the author state, "And then I drank a pot of coffee." For adventures and labors like Perry's, you don't need cups of coffee—you need pots of coffee. I even learned from Lloyd Perry the secret of making good coffee: don't use too much water!

A recurring theme in Perry's collection of stories is the concept of being a hand. Perry writes, "It's not possible to speak for all professing cowboys, however, I will stand up for the cowboy, who is called by other cowboys 'a hand.' To be ascribed the title of a hand is a very high honor among cowboys. This title has been handed down through the years, dating back to the first great American cowboy." As you read Perry's entertaining stories, along the way you will increase your understanding of what it is to be a hand, and you will increase your appreciation of what a distinct honor it is to be one. You will also be inspired by the unashamed testimony of a man who loves the LORD and is proud to be a Christian cowboy.

I am glad that I have read the stories of Lloyd Perry, and I am confident that you will be glad to read them too. I am proud that Mr. Perry is a friend of mine.

—Donald G. Baker
Professor Emeritus
Texas A&M University
College Station, Texas

INTRODUCTION
BY LYNN PERRY-HACKWORTH

$\mathcal{N}$ot too many people I know could ever write stories about events in their life and it turn out to be interesting or have a lasting impression. But as a kid, my brother, sisters, and I would hang on to every word our dad would be telling about the dog that was cut by a boar hog or the green horse that he'd been bucked off of, and I don't think I've ever once wondered, *What do other kids' dads do for a living?* Now that I'm grown, married, and have kids of my own, I've found myself once again eager to hear the stories about hunts, roundups, and long-gone (and sometimes unknown) family members through the letters that have come to the grandkids over the years. As my sister, Lee, and I have compiled these stories together into the forms of books, it has made us realize what a legacy our dad is giving us as a family. Theses old yarns, as Dad calls them, have faithfully bridged the miles over the years and given not only his grandkids and sons-in-laws a deeper understanding of who he is but also the sisters (Lynn, Lee, Jackie, and Amy Dale) as well.

Nowadays you don't hear about the old time cowboy living out his rough life in the Old West, and not many can recall the way of life "way back then" or would have wanted to live life by the standards of that time. But I must say I think I have witnessed it by viewing my dad's life. He's not much on the ways of today; in fact, I've often heard him say he thinks he was born a century too late. But he's not only a cowboy in word, body, heart, and soul but a Christian cowboy, a cowboy that gives God all the glory and isn't ashamed to tell you of his God as he tells you about a top dog or horse. Because as many of us have heard him say, "You take; if you can't give God the glory for what He's done, it ain't worth hearing or telling!" And that, folks, is what he has done for his family and is now sharing with you. I introduce to you a true example of a diamond in the rough, my dad, Mr. Lloyd Perry.

THE GREAT COMMISSION

And Jesus came and spake unto them, sayin, "All power is given unto me in heaven and in earth. Go ye therefore, and teach all nations, baptizing them in the name of the Father, and of the Son, and of the Holy Ghost: Teaching them to observe all things whatsoever I have commanded you: and, lo, I am with you always, even unto the end of the world."

Matthew 28:18–20 (KJV)

The local New Testament church is where God rules in the heart of his servants. The Great Commission was given to the church for the purpose of building God's kingdom.

A believer's testimony is our witness. It tells how we encountered a personal relationship with the LORD Jesus Christ in the new birth.

Discipleship is taught by example and by the holy Word of God as we live out the will of God in our life.

RUEL F. SANDERS
LAND, TIMBER & CATTLE
P. O. BOX 267   356-6006
MAGNOLIA, TEXAS 77355

293

BB-2015
1130

6-21- 19 81

$2550 00

PAY TO THE
ORDER OF   Lloyd Perry

two thousand five hundred fifty and /100   DOLLARS

GUARANTY BOND
PHONE A.C. 713-351-8821   State Bank
P. O. DRAWER J • TOMBALL, TEXAS 77375

Mrs Ruel F Sanders

Please - 1 Hereby

KNOW YOUR ENDORSER-REQUIRE IDENTIFICATION

PINELAND, TEXAS   Dec. 20,   19 80

PINELAND STATE BANK

BB-2319
1131

No. #201

PAY TO THE
ORDER OF   Lyold Perry $2000.00

Two thousand dollars and   no/100 DOLLARS

David Tabaka

FDIC

1-713-589-2922

⑈1131⊷2319⑈

#29-818-2

Operation Whitetail
Rt. 1 Box 75
Bronson, Texas 75930

DIAMOND IN THE ROUGH

$\mathcal{D}$iamonds in the rough are cowboys of vitality who have displayed the inborn chevalier of honor and respect (unwritten code of the West), cowboys who are born with the God-given ability of awareness, positioning, and timing, who have been tried and tested in the fire of time and are ascribed the title of being a hand by other old-time, cowboys. Every diamond in the rough has certain characteristics within his character that set him apart as a cut above the average. Younger cowboys, who have grown up under the influence of older cowboys, are not taught the common sense or good manners. These traits are expected to be lived out in every cowboy. Some of the other traits observed within a hand's (diamond in the rough's) character are the ability to be focused and stay in the ready.

Any cowboy in a crowd could be challenged by wild stock, but the point man and his backer are most often the hardest challenge. Often when wild stock runs, it has to be headed and turned by the point man and his backer. If the stock is on their left and the men are on the right, they're to head 'em and swing 'em left, as much as the stock will allow. The point man has to play off of the leader by positioning and repositioning several times as they gradually turn 'em left. He knows the moment the leader busts out of the bunch he's fixing to be tried. The cowboy gives ground as he pulls the left rein of his bridle and spurs the left side of the horse (this is a cue for the horse to look at the stock and pick up speed as they fade back to the right). This all happens fast. If the stock wants to go right, the cowboy holds his horse a little back, forcing the stock to commit out in front of the horse and rider. If the rider and the horse face up on the stock, they will lose their momentum and are apt to have all of the stock scattered to the four winds.

It makes sense, for in life we all face serious trials, and rarely do we get second chances. So we have to be aware and reposition ourselves by being led by God's Spirit through his lordship in our lives. This way, we can all shine as diamonds in the rough.

CRYBABY

Anybody that knows me knows that I can barely read writing or write reading.

I was backed into writing down some old yarns for my grandchildren, who, according to my daughter Lora Lee, said, "Dad, they want to know you. I came to realize I don't know you. I don't think any of your children know you. As far as that goes, I don't think anyone really knows you."

I just grunted at that and said, "Miss knowing me, you ain't missing much. Miss knowing God, and you missed it all."

Lee said, "I know what you mean, Dad, but we'd appreciate it if you'd help us to know something about you."

All I said was, "We'll see."

Now, it spooks my mule if I go to bragging on myself or the things dear to me. Then the thought came to me: use what God has laid into your hand and brag on Jesus, for He's the only one worth bragging on anyway.

It was the next week while I was hunting that I came by the place where I liked to have gotten killed by roping a cow a few years before. I thought about it, and the purpose for God sparing me had to be for me to serve Him. That night I wrote it down. Three or four days later, Lee called me, crying.

I said, "Heey . . . , I don't like a crybaby. Now, what's wrong?"

Lee said, "Dad, I didn't know. Why didn't you tell someone?"

I said, "It's all passed. It happened a long time ago. It's nothing to get upset about. Furthermore, if you're going to be a crybaby, I won't write anymore."

She said, "Dad, we all love you. Don't you know that?"

Now, Lee didn't know it, but that liked to have made a crybaby out of me.

COLD, HARD CASH

After having moved off and leaving the old Lone Star State, I finally realized that I just wasn't strong enough to break the ties that bind. My youthful, lustful yondering had eventually become the whip of life. I missed mostly Mom and Dad, and I'd get me a bad case of the down-yonders. I'd look around at my trade stock, load a couple of horses, and go a-trading. It would sometimes take me five to ten days to get traded out, for I was hung with the responsibility and the obligation to provide for a family. So I was usually gone about a week, or until I got weak, whichever the case.

In my travels on the 350-mile journey south, I'd gotten acquainted with a few folks along life's highway. It's about as important to remember whom you know as what you've seen or to remember what you know someone is looking for. I've often said that success is over the long haul, not misrepresenting your stock. It's important that you're a horseman if you're in this business, for you'll come up against the best. A good horseman knows it takes miles and miles of wet saddle pads as well as the breeding and training of an honest using horse. If you're horseman enough you learn shortcuts in order to make 'em show and not tell much. I call it "dressing 'em up." I find trading a lot like fighting. I know how it goes but was never very good at it, but like a steer, I tried.

I'd gotten acquainted on first-name basis with an old-time horse trader, Mr. Grady Stephens. I don't know why I liked this old, long, crooked-nosed scoundrel; he could usually outtrade me and told me a couple of times, "I'd rather beat you in a trade than anybody."

I came back with, "Why, you old, sorry, lowlife, long, crooked-nosed scoundrel! Why do you want to beat me so bad?"

He'd laugh and say, "Because it hurts you worse than anybody... that I know." I didn't like it, but I was young and took some ragging if I liked 'em. If I didn't like 'em, I'd get away from 'em quick and wouldn't say a word.

It was a known fact to me that Grady had gotten full worth out of a few horses that he'd either traded or sold me. One day he said to me, "If you take this horse and sell him to someone else for more money than you paid me, then you done cheated... somebody." Now, I was young and had it to prove. I intended to earn their respect by trading with 'em, taking their stock, and then outtrading 'em. Then smile and make 'em like it. Now I had my work cut out for me, for that's a big, tall order, a mouthful, and hard to do.

It was known that Grady had a customer with a high-dollar surrey (one horse-drawn fancy buggy) and was looking for a gentle shaft horse to pull this rig. Word was that he'd bought one horse at a horse sale that was misrepresented and wasn't a shaft horse. That horse had bucked and kicked and had scarred up this customer's surrey. Now, I knew of an honest shaft horse that was old and poor, but I didn't want to tie up my trade money in such a risky deal. I'd never been a middleman before, but Grady agreed to pay me one hundred dollars if he bought this horse for telling him the owner's name. I went to the man selling this horse and told him I had a buyer and that he was going to give me a hundred dollars for selling this horse. Like I've always said, it's sometimes whom you know and not always what you know that can make a difference. However, trading does beat working.

Grady purposely waited to come look at this horse until the day before the monthly horse sale in Wister, Oklahoma. He drug his foot, acting like he didn't think this horse would suit the deal. He found all kinds of faults with this horse, some I thought he probably made up. I nearly had to swallow my tongue to keep from interfering in their business. Finally, when the man said, "That's all right; I'll take him to the horse sale tomorrow," Grady told him he'd try to help him all he could.

It was fairly easy to see through this deal. Grady not only knocked me out of one hundred dollars for selling the horse for this fellow, but he was going to buy the horse cheaper through the sale barn. Then he'd leave from there without paying me the one hundred dollars too! He'd just knocked the middleman out of two hundred dollars (a hundred for finding the horse (for the buyer) and a hundred for selling the horse (for the seller) by sayin' that he bought this horse in the sale barn. All of a sudden I didn't like being a middleman, especially after I couldn't convince this fellow that if he didn't take the horse to the sale the next day Grady would be back to buy this shaft horse and that we would get the price that he had first priced this horse for. I said to this fellow, "If it was me, I'd play hardball and raise the price one hundred dollars."

This fellow just looked at me and said, "Do declare! I don't know about all this, but I believe I'd better let this ol' hoss go."

Grady bought three head of horses. One of them was the shaft horse, and like I had figured it all along, that ol' scoundrel got away without paying me a dime.

Now it was a couple of weeks before I got a case of the down-yonders. In fact, I didn't have a trade horse when I blew into Grady's town. When he saw me he was all smiles, hand-shaking, and talking on like I was some kind of kin. I was polite and thought I'd give him enough rope to hang himself, but if he didn't hang himself, then I was right ready to do the hanging myself.

He was talking and brushing the back of a wired mare (old wire scars) that he'd bought up at the Oklahoma horse sale two weeks before. He said, "You ought to ride this mare; she's the brokest, most honest horse that's been on this place for a while."

I grunted and said, "If she's honest, then that's more than I'd say for the fellow that owns her."

He laughed and said, "I didn't buy that shaft horse from your man; I bought him out of the sale barn, so be a good sport and don't be a bad loser."

"I ain't no loser. I got cheated, plum robbed."

He handed me the reins and tried changing the subject by saying, "Ride this mare, and let's go to Waco tonight to a horse sale."

"Waco! I ain't even got a trade horse."

"I've been trying to get you to ride this one. You can own her cheap."

"Wait a minute. Either you ain't hearing or you ain't understanding, because I ain't going nowhere with you. Now I may have been born in the night, but not last night, for I must have 'easy' written on me for you to think I'd buy a wired-up mare that you couldn't get on and ride fast enough to give to anyone else."

He just stood there shaking his head like a bull and said, "Ride the horse."

Now as I walked her off slowly, she gathered and came back under herself without asking anymore than just a light neck rein. I slow-loped her, then rolled her over both sides of her hocks left and right, then sped her up, and slid an eleven out in some sandy ground. I stepped off and handed him the reins and said, "She's nice."

He said, "Go to Waco, and I'll take my money back on her."

"Less the one hundred dollars that you owe me."

"All right! All right! Give me $200 before I change my mind."

Now I flat enjoyed riding this mare; she just didn't make many (or any) mistakes. After getting to Waco, I noticed a few folks were watching us in the parking lot at the horse sale, so I gave them a dose of what they'd come to see, since this mare could naturally ride around. When I rode the mare into the ring that night, she was still hot and wet with sweat, and I figured that I was one of the most impressed people there. When the auctioneer asked me if I had anything to say, I said, "Nope! This kind speaks for themselves." Now, I never said another word, for I knew they saw all the mare's wired scars. So just before they sold me out for six hundred fifty dollars, I hollered, "Worth more! PO!"

Somebody came back with, "How much?"

I said, "Eight hundred fifty dollars and not a dime less."

Grady was standing there beside the ring and said to me, "Don't be a hog and act crazy."

I smiled at him and said it again: "Eight hundred fifty dollars and not one dime less."

So I PO'd my wired mare and left Waco at about 3:00 a.m.

About the time I was getting in the next morning with my horse, Dad was getting up. So I helped 'em drink a pot of coffee and told him and Mom I needed a couple hours' rest. After that I'd be ready to go help 'em until noon. After Mom, Dad, and I ate dinner, I went looking for a buyer. I'd heard about a misplaced Arkie (Arkansas) carpenter who'd turned cowboy and was managing a large ranch in the Navasota river bottom.

I found this old boy hard at work, and after we'd visited for about five minutes, I said, "Are you looking for a sure-nuff, good-using horse ... cheap?"

He was grinning like an opossum that had eaten a green persimmon when he said, "Now, how did you know?"

I didn't say nothing smart like "a bird told me." What I said was, "This is a big ranch; I didn't figure you'd walk these cattle into a pen afoot." After we'd talked a little while, I said, "I didn't bring my trailer, or I would have had this horse with me. If you've got the time, you're welcome to come over and try her. If you like her, we will figure out something."

He said, "The ranch has got a truck and trailer. But if it's all the same to you, I'll come try her first. If I like her I'll come back with a truck and trailer and pick her up later."

Now after he'd ridden the mare around about fifteen minutes, he came up to me and said, "How much for the mare?"

I smiled and said, "Eight hundred fifty dollars."

He asked, "Is that your low dollar?"

"Yes, sir. Eight hundred fifty dollars and not a dime less."

"Well, I'll take her."

"All right, let's go get that truck and trailer."

He came back with, "How about tomorrow?"

"I do business at the Bedias Baptist Church tomorrow. I do my trading on Monday through Saturday."

He smiled and said, "I need a little time to raise that much money. How about after church, say one o'clock? I can be here with the cold, hard cash." He then said something about having to work and that he wouldn't be able to come until Monday evening; that is, if we couldn't do business the next day.

I said, "I'll be here tomorrow at one o'clock then."

He was early. I had just gotten in from church and had the mare caught as he was driving up. After we loaded the mare, he went around on the passenger side of his truck. I thought he was going for his pen and checkbook. As he opened the door he took out a small, white flour sack. When I started to say, "Is that your money?" I realized that it was the money! I shook my head and said, "Man! I ain't never sold a horse for gold!"

He said, "It ain't gold, but it's cold, hard cash. I didn't plan on buying a horse until after I'd gotten paid my first paycheck, but I know you. That horse and you won't wait. The money is all there if you want to count it."

I smiled and said, "Friend, I'll take your word."

On my way back north to Talihina, Oklahoma, I couldn't help but stop by Grady's and tell him that I'd sold the mare. I thought about asking Grady if he'd help me count my money. But before saying much more, I thought the better of it. I'd better not try rubbing salt in an open wound. I would just show him the sack of gold and smiled real big. That would be good enough.

WILD BOAR BAGGED IN RIVER BOTTOM SAFARI

V. T. WILLIAMS, Lloyd Perry and Jim Bay pose with the 425-pound wild boar which they captured and killed early Thursday morning on the W. C. Mitchell Ranch in the Navasota River bottom. A hog has been on the Mitchell Ranch for a long time and it would be difficult to estimate the damage it has done to large coastal Bermuda pasture. Other hunters have tried in vain to locate this

THINGS DON'T ALWAYS
GO LIKE THEY SHOULD

From the time of my early childhood, I'd ridden horseback for miles and miles wondering how I'd ever cowboy out a living without taking somebody's wages. I knew I had to have a rig and a setup, and someday maybe a family. I was never secure in my life's plan and felt that I had 'er made, but I was rather inconsiderably tight with a dollar and felt that I got it to make. In this news clipping I was barely nineteen years old, lost and without God, barely six months after a bad rodeo accident where I'd liked to have gotten killed, and a week after me and my fiancée had broken our engagement. Now things ain't ever as bad as they could be, but I didn't believe that it could get much worse. So I keep this old newspaper clipping as a reminder that sometimes when it rains, it pours.

The Mitchell Ranch had, at one time, been owned by Mr. Knox Williams, whose son, Mr. Slone Williams, grew up with Mr. E.E. Allen Jr. Mr. Slone Williams was a rodeo producer, and Jr. picked up at the local rodeos. Jr. is a second cousin of mine, an old-time cowboy who made an impression in my life growing up, for he was an extremely good hand. Now, a large tract of land north of the

Mitchell Ranch was owned by Jr.'s dad and was part of their estate. Jr. and Mr. Mitchell had a partnership on several head of cattle. Jim Bay and I grew up together and were acquainted with Mr. V.T. Williams, who was a pipe fitter and weekend warrior hog hunter.

At seventeen years old, I owned my first rig (truck, trailer, and a string of horses and dogs). I had picked up Jimmy and V.T. at 5:00 a.m. to go hog hunting. We'd gotten to the Mitchell Ranch at daylight, and Jr. had left the front gate unlocked and was waiting with his horse saddled to show us where this hog had been rooting. The dogs found this hog in less time than it takes to tell it. The hog was lying close to the rooting in a thicket next to a branch (small waterway). When the hog moved, I saw it wasn't a cold-blooded hog but rather a good-blooded, short-nosed, red Duoc hog that was worth over one hundred dollars. I said to Jimmy, "Let's catch him," for that was the purpose of Jimmy and I going on this hog hunt. As we were moving into the thicket, the hog ran out of the brush at a dog. Mr. Williams saw the size of that hog and his teeth and came out with some kind of an old pistol and shot him from the back of his horse, killing a one-hundred dollar hog graveyard dead.

In cowboy terminology, a hundred-dollar bill amounted to four hard days of day work. This hog amounted to nothing dead, except more work. Now, a young hand might say, "Damn," but he'd best not say anything more.

THREE DAYS WEST
OF SINGLETON

*E*very now and then I get the urge to spin a tale, but I have to put a warning label on my tales. I believe they call them "Westerns." My daughter, Lee, said to me, "Dad, you're the one who told us that if it's not true, it's not worth telling." This tale ain't worth telling, but the thing is, it helps get me "kick-started."

It was after Thanksgiving, and I knew it wouldn't be long until Christmas. So I thought about getting this gal I knew a Christmas present. But folks this day and time don't be lacking for much of anything, and that made it difficult for me to know what to get her. I went to town and went by Walmart Fall Apart thinking I'd do a little fingerprinting around (you know, pick it up, look at it, then put it back); I had plenty of time to buy something later.

Now, I was pretty sure that I looked plum out of place in the women's department, but they were busy, so I stood around until I finally had a chance to say something to this gal wearing a blue jacket that said "I Can Help." So I said, "Ma'am?"

She turned around and gave me a looking over and said, "What ... do ... you ... want?"

Now I ain't much of a hand at talking to the ladies, but I thought that she spoke a little rude to a cash-paying customer. I tried to overlook it, so I said, "Ma'am, I'm looking for a gift for a lady. Can you help me?"

"How about a dress?" I nodded my head yes, and she asked, "What color?"

"Red."

"What size?"

"Ma'am, I ain't got a clue. She's about your height and build."

She went through a bunch of clothes and came up with one and held it out in front of her. I noticed she and the dress both looked pretty good. So I nodded my head yes.

As an afterthought I asked, "How much?"

She just flipped the price tag around there at me. It was eighty-nine dollars, and she said, "Plus tax."

I asked, "Ma'am, can we look at something else?"

She folded it up and put it all back and said, "Follow me. How about a bottle of perfume?"

I nodded my head—that was okay. She went behind the counter and got a bottle, put some on her wrist, and said, "Le Pariee."

It smelled okay, so I said, "How much?"

"Sixty-five dollars per ounce."

I raised up my arm, bowed my head over and kinda snorted, then said, "Three days west of Singleton. It don't cost a dime!"

Now I knew better than to have done that, so I hung my head down and said, "Ma'am, I'm sorry, but you got me all wrong. I'm just looking for something cheap."

She didn't say a word, just made a fist and with her index finger motioned for me to follow her. She went down to where they had the women's hairbrushes, and when she got to the hand mirrors, she shoved that hand mirror in front of my face and said, "Why don't you look at that?" and walked off. Imagine that!

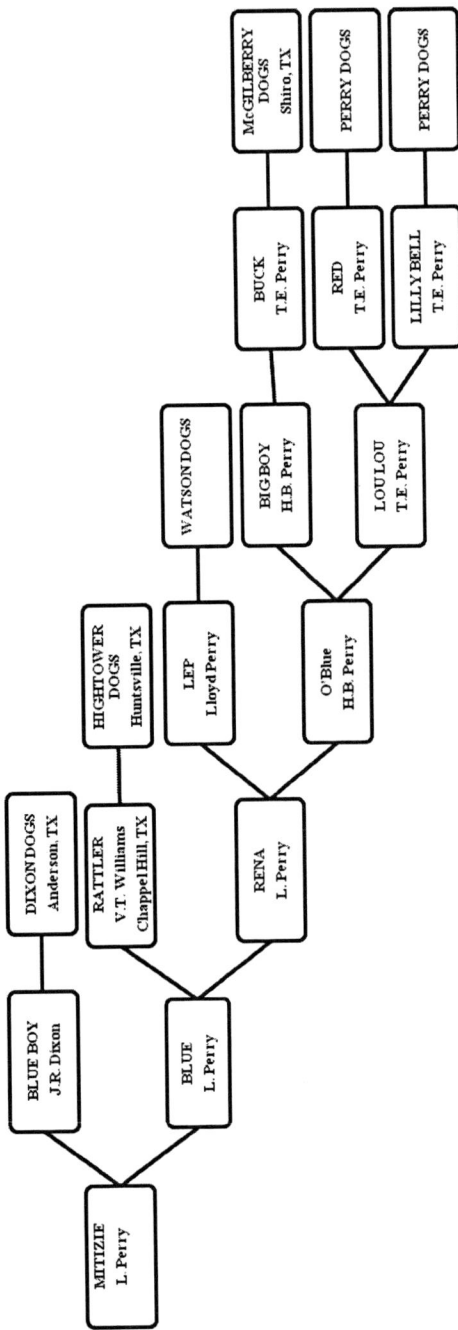

OL' MITZIE
FIRST EXCEPTIONALLY GOOD TOP DOG

I was only five years old when my dad gave me my first puppy. It was only three weeks old, and Dad didn't expect him to live. Dad had found a dead gray fox behind the barn where old Lilly Bell had whelped. Dad figured Ol' Lilly Bell had killed the fox and that it was rabid. Dad tied Ol' Lilly Bell on the inside of his corn crib and waited several days before she went rabid. I remembered how it hurt Dad to have to put her down, and those old bygone memories never fade away.

I raised one pup out of the litter that I called Smokey. He went everywhere I went horseback. I was seven years old when we were living in Anderson, Texas, on my grandmother Perry's property. I was in school when Ol' Smokey took rabies, and my mother had to put him down. That was tough on her and me. Mom loved a good dog. And I don't remember many sorry dogs that got to stay around our house and eat Mom's scalded cornmeal that was ground especially for them.

In 1963, I had three horses in my string and three dogs that I used both ways (cows and hogs). In November Ol' Blue whelped one pup out of Mister J.R. Dickson's dog that I called Mitzie. There's something a little different about an exceptionally good dog that a cowboy is able to pick up on even when they are young. A cowboy that is a hand looks for that same natural ability that makes him a cut above within a dog or horse. At a tender age he can tell, without seeing the whole picture, if he thinks a dog or horse has this ability to be an exceptionally good top dog. Only time will tell for sure.

I have raised a lot of puppies from the time I was five years old until I was twenty-five years old. Ol' Mitzie was different in everything she did. By the time she was a year and a half old, she was an exceptionally good cow dog. And by the time she was two years old, she was an exceptional hog dog as well as a tree dog. She not only done all three jobs well, she made it look easy.

Before I got Ol' Mitzie, I was beginning to see part of my dream come true. In 1963 I bought my first new rig. I was working the Huntsville sale barn for Mr. Sonny Moore, one day a week and doing day work. Screwworms were extremely bad; therefore, my employment stayed steady through the summer and fall. Common labor was making five dollars a day, and I charged twenty-five dollars a day, taking cowboy wages for me, my horse, and dogs. Folks back then expected you to do the work of three people, so you'd better have a horse that could cover a cow like sunshine and a string of dogs that were way above average. The jobs that a cowboy got back then were usually the jobs that someone had already messed up by spoiling these cattle to where they couldn't pen them. If I took a job and spent all day and couldn't pen any of the cattle, then I didn't get any pay; however, most of the time I got part or the majority of the cattle penned. And if the owner wanted these other cattle roped, then it was understood that I got paid by the head for the cattle that I caught. These terms and conditions were always understood up front. I worked alone, and I understood it wasn't going to be easy, but if you couldn't handle the heat, then stay out of the kitchen.

Ol' Mitzie came into my life in the late 1960s. She was a one-man dog, and it seemed she always tried extremely hard to please.

Often, when I got spoiled cattle that didn't want to take the gate, she would leave the front end of the cattle and the other dogs coming to me as I called her by name and repeatedly saying "Load 'em." That little extra made Ol' Mitzie a cut above the average. She was my first extremely good top dog.

When I was twenty-eight years old, I'd bought a two-year-old dog called Ol' Jr. from Mr. Billy Williams. Ol' Jr. was way too rough for a cow dog. I used him on hogs, and he became an exceptionally good tree dog. Back then there was a place for a rough dog, and there's a place and time when a rough dog is what you've got to have to do a job. Most of the time, if I kept adding mild dogs, they would eventually do the job of a rough dog.

Over the next several years, I mated Ol' Mitzie to Ol' Jr., and all of their puppies were black dogs that were a little above average. Over time they became known as "Perry dogs."

It is not unusual for two cowboys to sit and talk for an hour or two about the genealogies of different old horses or dogs. I am often asked about different old-timers that had a string of dogs or horses that carried the owner's last name or about a string of horses that carried a certain stud horse's bloodline name. Any hand is never content. He will always be looking for something a little better than what he's riding or what's following him. This is just the cowboy way.

In the 1970s, coon hides had gone up for a couple of years in a row. After starting Ol' Mitzie to tree coons, I began hunting with her and Ol' Jr. along with a trapline. With winter being a slow time for a day hand, this trapping and hunting helped me to subsidize my income. One season I sold over three thousand dollars' worth of hides. This impressed my dad, for he believed that a person was fortunate to have only owned one exceptionally good dog in a lifetime.

In 1996, I was fifty-one years old and had only had one extremely good top dog. Over the years since God brought me to the end of myself, I've had five more. I was impressed that as a Christian I'm to do all to the glory of God. The Bible says in 1 Corinthians 10:31 (KJV), "Whether therefore ye eat or drink or whatsoever ye do, do all to the glory of God." When the Spirit impressed God's Word upon my mind, I asked, "LORD, how do I do this? How do I, a cowboy, do all to the glory of God?" As I sat there in my simplicity, I felt impressed to give all the credit to God. I find this to be a battle between the Spirit and my flesh, for I often find it hard to give all credit to God; therefore, I often say, "Thank you, LORD." In the passing of years I try to make it a point to credit God for the blessings that he has placed in my hand. I've tried to use my horses and dogs as a tool in showing the incredible difference God makes in a personal relationship as LORD of life.

From my youth until I was twenty-five years old, I raised several dogs. Ol' Mitzie was my first extremely good top dog, and for the next twenty-six years I never raised another dog that was equal. Immediately after I began to get things God's way, giving God credit, God placed into my hands Ol' Bunt, and after Ol' Bunt, Ol' Lou II, Ol' CC Rider, Ol' Skitty, and Ol' Sue Baby II, all exceptionally good top dogs. All of these dogs are descendants of Ol' Mitzie and were one-man dogs. All were black except Sue Baby II.

WE'RE BOTH PERRYS

A couple of railroader friends of mine, Mr. Rabie Rallan and his son, Daniel, went on a big mule deer hunt way up in Canada. Now, they had a hunting guide who took them back in the cold wilds of that north country where they hunted and camped for several days and nights. Both of these railroaders are good one-shot hunters who've gone hog hunting with me a few times in the past. Hog hunting and catching (taking them alive) is close, hard work. It's not like shooting a hog from a distance. When the dogs have the hog bayed up and you have to crawl into a thicket, you are getting close to your work.

The hog market on live hogs had gone back up in 2005 and 2006, and me and a couple of my young pards (cowboys) were catching 'em alive and selling to a couple of game ranches (hunting outfits) for a little over the market price. Shortly after the opening of hog season (the day after deer season closes), this old, retired railroader called me and asked if it was possible that I could take him, his son, and a friend on a little hog hunt. I usually try to accommodate folks; but I told him the market is up on live hogs, and when you kill one, you got to clean it, get it on ice, take it to someone who really don't want to buy it anyways, and then wait on your money. He said he understood where I was coming from and that this friend had never seen hogs caught and that it would be even more exciting to a fellow from way up north, Canada.

Now, I ain't the sharpest knife in the drawer, but I ain't the dullest either. Something about this deal didn't add up because this old railroader pretty much thought that anyone who crawled in on a wild hog lived to the beat of another drummer. Why all of a sudden from crazy to exciting? When I got to asking questions, I found out this friend of theirs was a Canadian hunting guide, and this is the way that I read the rest of the story between the lines.

This old Texas railroader, who was stuck way off in that cold north country, got to missing the warm, sunny, old Lone Star State. Sitting around one of them cold, lonely campfires at night, he probably got to thinking about all that exciting café socializing that he did and was missing it. Having no one to talk to but this unlearned Canadian guide, who had never hunted or caught a wild Russian boar hog, the old Texas railroader probably embellished the size of a wild boar hog. One thing's for certain: whatever he said must have excited this hunting guide enough that he put up hard-earned money for an airplane ticket to come all the way to Texas just to have a look-see. That got me to wondering about those Canadian folk, if they were that curious or whether the hunting guides just made that much money. I finally decided that this hunting guide probably had made enough extra money off these ol' railroaders for a trip to the old west.

The Texas cowboy in me didn't want to let this old Texas railroader down by not being able to show this northern former Canadian hunting guide something he wouldn't soon forget about being here in Texas, the Old Wild West. But here in the real world, it don't always happen just that way. You can't make a thing happen out of the clear blue.

It would have been a normal, clear, cold day in January, except those railroaders wanted to start the day at about four o'clock in the morning. I thought I'd told 'em I had some pretty good dogs and that if they couldn't wait for the sun to come up, at least wait until it got light enough to see. But I got called out of my sack early, and I thought no better of getting lil Hersh up. Lil Hersh is my brother's grandson; he's one of my pards that's quite a hand. I don't know what kin that makes us. All I know is we're both Perrys.

We got to the lake at the breaking of the cold, gray dawn. I was all bundled up on my four-wheeler, with a young dog riding behind me. Lil Hersh had a young dog and a bulldog riding behind him. We both had a "strike dog" a-loose and had moved about a half mile when our dogs began to pick up hog sign (trail). We then turned our two young dogs a-loose. I sent all the younger men west around Cedar Creek's inlet. The dogs bayed, and three Maverick boar hogs broke before the young men were able to get in position. A two-hundred-pound boar hog crossed the narrowest part of the inlet going west in front of me. While I was going north to a crossing, I saw another big hog going north across open country. Now the boar hog that the dogs were running went west and didn't run over a quarter mile. When he ran into another bunch of family hogs (sows and shoats), the hogs busted the bay, scattering our dogs to the four winds. We spent a couple hours catching two shoats and one poor sow that wasn't worth over thirty or forty dollars.

I got my dogs stopped and lil Hersh had his young dog caught, but the older gyp that used to belong to my older brother Hershel wouldn't let him catch her. So we pulled out going back east from off Plum Creek and back toward Cedar Creek, where I'd seen the other big boar hog. Hersh kept calling this ol' gyp. We'd seen her cross an opening headed back east, the way the bunch of hogs had been laying at the first. We'd gotten back to where I'd seen this big hog going north. I had dropped my dogs down, and they were beginning to smell the hog sign and fixing to pull freight. Then lil Hersh's ol' gyp bayed. My dogs stopped their trailing and honored her. In five minutes we were headed back to Plum Creek, where we'd just come from. I managed to get positioning on Plum Creek this time with my crew lined out to cut the hog off and kill him.

Now, if you crawl into a thicket where you can hardly see, and if two hundred pounds of hog looks big, one that weighs three hundred pounds looks like a bull. Lil Hersh said to me over the hand radio, "You'd better get over here; he's big." As we moved in, I put my gun up and noticed the Canadian did likewise, but he soon had some kind of camera in his hands and wasn't thinking about helping us catch this hog.

We walked from our four-wheelers and had just gotten to the edge of where thick briers, yaupon, and undergrowth got real thick. We had come a little ways off Plum Creek, for the hog had been headed that way. I'd just said to Hersh that I was here when this hog ran at a dog and stopped within eight or ten feet in front of me. I'd stepped beside a tree about the time the bulldog caught this hog, and there was a lot of thrashing going on. As I looked around, I didn't see any backers anymore, but I managed to get both hands around one back leg and get it up. The other hind leg was up off the ground, and this big hog had leaving on his mind. He jerked me back and forth and had pulled me several feet through some bad stuff. Hersh was there, but because of a tree and thick brush, he couldn't get a front leg and get this hog over on his side. So I said, "Forget the front leg! Help me!" When Daniel showed up—he was some kind of stout from that railroad work, handling those heavy cross ties—he grabbed that other leg, and the hog came back with very little help from me. Hersh had a front leg and laid that hog on his side.

Now, a lot of cowboys have got a little, low laugh that most folks are apt to miss. He'll only make this little laugh when he's cut, or caught, a big hog. It goes, *He-he-he-hee*. Both of us Perrys laughed. I laughed again at that Canadian taking pictures as I backed up to a pine tree and sat down on the ground and quickly said, "Thank you, LORD, lest I forget and think it was just out of the clear blue."

I only smiled again when this old railroader, Rabie, said to the Canadian, "I told you! They do it all the time!"

I got one last little laugh and said, "Thank you, LORD," when I sold that hog for one hundred fifty dollars to Mr. Joe Langley, who runs a game ranch in Centerville, Texas.

HUMANS

I've never been much of a people person, and neither have my old, crazy dogs. Some of my old horses would have been hard for a stranger to catch and would have rollers (a sound in their nostrils). However, my old dogs would bark and try to get away from a stranger. If they were tied, they'd stand their ground or get into their dog house and bark. For years I called this my trademark, but it could be the character of the man passed on to the animal through training and the winning of confidence as they spend time alone together.

A fellow from East Texas called me and said that I was recommended to him as having trained and sold some good dogs at a high-price shop. In September of 2002 in the middle of the week, early one morning, me and this fellow made a little hunt. It had rained a few days before, but we hunted over two hours and never found any fresh hog sign. I thought about some sign I'd seen at a deer feeder the week before as I was looking for a couple of my escaped sale barn cows. I told this fella, "About three miles from here I saw some sign fresh at a deer feeder last week." I loaded my dogs, Ol' To-To-Lou and Ol' Gurdie, on my four-wheeler, and we took off.

It was about 11:00 a.m. when I'd seen some sign of family hogs (sow and pigs) about a quarter of a mile from this feeder. I unloaded the two dogs, and they began working this sign. In about ten minutes they bayed. I thought it was strange that these hogs would be around that feeder in the middle of the day. We took off toward my dogs. When I came out of the woods to this the feeder, I saw a man with something in his hand, and those two dogs had 'em bayed up. As I rode up I said, "Hey…a…a…aa," and the dogs both came to me and jumped up on my four-wheeler. I snapped them and said, "Mister, I'm sorry about this. They didn't bite you, did they?"

This older fellow said, "No, sir, I'm not bit."

"I feel bad about this, sir. I didn't know anyone was in here. Those dogs left on hog sign."

"It's all right, Mr. Perry. Hogs have been all around my feeder, and I was afraid they'd turn it over and tear something up, so I came down this morning to stake it down. I just got here when your dogs took to me."

Now, I was surprised that he knew who I was, for I'd never met or seen this fellow. Then my crazy, warped sense of humor caused me to think about Aubrey Love telling a tale. Aubrey had a good meat dog, and we'd killed a lot of birds over this ol' gyp. It was some years later that Aubrey said that he went to Anderson and his ol' dog had jumped into his truck and went with him. Aubrey was visiting on the street when he'd noticed that his dog had jumped out of his truck and had thrown down on point, pointing this fellow. Aubrey stepped over and placed his hand upon this dog and said to the feller, "Mister, are you a bird hunter?" The feller answered, "No." He said, "Have you by chance happened to have been around some quail?" He said, "No." Aubrey hung his head down and said, "Mister, I apologize for my dog's rude behavior." He then stuck out his hand and said, "I'm Aubrey Love." The feller answered, "My name is Bob White." (This might be a tale, for Aubrey and his cousin, Earl White, could really tell 'em and keep you laughing.)

But I didn't figure this old fellow was in any mood for any nonsense. So I never said what I was thinking. I just stuck my hand out and said, "I'm Lloyd Perry." We shook hands, and he told me his name (I forget, but it wasn't "Hog"). I asked, "How is it you know my name?"

"Mr. Perry, a couple of years ago you had a run-in with one of my hunters. He is no longer on this lease. That fellow was a highway patrolman, and he found your truck and got your license plate number and name. He wanted Mr. Jake Howard to file charges on you, but Mr. Howard said that you hunted on all his property and wouldn't do it."

I hung my head down and said, "Mister, I'm sorry about that too, but that fellow didn't bridle me correctly (approach me in the right way). It's true I was following my old dogs and we came across this place, but the dogs were bayed across the fence in another place. He was sitting there next to the fence in his truck when he seen me and came to meet me. I threw up my hand to speak and go on to my dogs when he said, 'Hey you! Stop there! What's your name? What are you doing in here? Don't you know this place is under lease?' I only smiled and said, 'Mister, you sure ask a lot of questions, especially to a stranger.' I gave no other answer and started on to my dogs. He said, 'Are you going to answer or do I have to take this to Mr. Howard?'"

This older fellow said, "Mr. Perry, I'm retired and live in Bryan, Texas. I've leased this place for eighteen years. I've known where you live and who you are for a long time. Mr. Howard said you would be in here anytime but not in deer season, and that's good enough for me."

I said, "Mister, I hope me and my dogs can stay out of your way. Again, I'm sorry about all this."

We shook hands and drove off; however, I don't think this potential hog dog buyer was really interested in trying these dogs anymore. He was looking for a hog dog and not a human dog.

Home Sweet Home

Lloyd Perry
Singleton, Tex.

HUNT OR PLAY

We had had some unusual fall-type mornings with the temperatures down in the sixties. That's unusual for late June, early July in Texas. With this kind of weather, a man with any hunt in him ought to be in the woods. But there I was working on my stock pens and holding trap. Couldn't hunt, for all my old dogs had what I thought was a kennel cough but turned out to be some kind of pneumonia.

Now it was really hard for me to stay hooked up, with it being such a good morning, but I stuck it out until noon. Before going to the house, I went to the garden and picked a bucket of tomatoes. When I got to the house, I found all the rest of the vegetables either needed to be canned or thrown out. Knowing this little job would take the rest of the day and into the night, an old saying came to mind. Something 'bout a woman's work being from sun to sun but a man's work is never done. I pulled the door shut behind me as I stepped into the house. I thought it had been quite a while since I'd seen a sun-to-sun woman. They must have quit making that model.

In a domino game I may have let the cat out of the bag, in a roundabout way, in a conversation with a lady when I said, "I prefer a woman partner in a domino tournament. Especially one who likes to win and plays like she has something to prove in a hard-fought match. When a partner works to exhaustion and doesn't snap under the tension, I know that she's played her heart out."

I know all too well how hard it is to win confidence. It doesn't matter if it's a domino partner or weather; it's a bond between my horse or dog. There comes a time when they believe in you and trust you. You have to prove up that you're real also. This has always been my stock and trade—push to the limit, keep a low profile, using only soft words, yet able to hold a firm yet gentle hand. It's God who has given me the ability to hold up my end of the deal, that I might bring glory unto my Savior and LORD Jesus Christ in whatever I do. If I give God the credit, it glorifies Him and not me.

EARLY RISE/LATE FALL

*N*ow, I had been riding a good-looking, eight-year-old Bert-bred gelding that handled himself well and could spook to a cow. Then all of a sudden, all the wheels ran off of my life, and my whole world came undone in a divorce. After everything was all said and done, it was still my name that was signed to a sizable note at the bank. It's the code of the West that if you make a debt, you owe a debt. It would have been easier, and a whole lot less trouble, to have just let the bank assume that collateral. But that's not my way. So in order to leave respectfully, I had nothing to do but pay up. Now, it's a known fact that when a cowboy has to sell his horse in order to leave town, it's time to get out of Dodge.

In 1993 these new-fangled cell phones were something relatively new to me. Phones, along with all luxuries, carry an expense. However, when I made it back to Texas and set up shop, it wasn't real handy scheduling my appointments to do day work. Unless I ran into someone who needed my employment around a sale barn, they'd have to call one of my brothers, my brothers would have to get me the message, and then I'd call them back. I was informed that I was missing a lot of business by not having a cell phone. I only smiled and said, "You might be right." If inconvenience caused me any loss of work, I figured I could do without that account, for it would take at least a couple of extra days' work to pay the bill each month.

After having thought on it some, I realized I might have reacted a little hastily; basically I was already working at a disadvantage. I was riding one of two colts that I had left and didn't own a cow dog; therefore, I didn't have much in the way of services to offer anyone.

The two colts that I had left went back four generations on the mare side of horses that I owned. The two-year-old colt was a horse colt that wasn't broke. The three-year-old was a filly I had just begun riding that I called Easter. I didn't exactly like riding a mare, but I didn't have any choice. She'd been ridden a few times but was a lot like me; she didn't know much.

Some who don't really know me would think my work ethics aren't that good. It's common among my kind to be looking for a job when we find one, and if things don't shape up to suit us, we'll move on. It won't be because of hard work. I've been fortunate to be able to do my job, but I won't do my job and somebody else's too. I find when you do somebody else's work, it soon gets to be your work. I'd rather be alone than with someone who can't cut the mustard.

Any hand knows when he's in the company of other hands, for the challenge becomes a performance. The only compliment he's apt to receive is a smile or that little laugh that goes *He-he-hee.* But unless I forget and fail to give credit and all glory to God, knowing that without Him I can do nothing, I say, "Thank you, LORD Jesus."

I was needing employment when my brother Hershel said he had a week's work for me. There were six of us working in this cow crowd on the old Walden Ranch in the Brazos River bottom. Most all of the bottom land on this old ranch was in cultivation except for the low, wet, swampy part that had some high ground covered with timber, brush, and wild roses. Across this old tram were the working pens with a couple hundred acres of good bottom grasslands they called the trap pasture. Most of the rest of this upland was old sandy fields with some thick timber and yaupon in places. One of these old fields had a good fence, and ponds were made in some of these deep gullies. We'd spent two days pushing cattle into this trap. The third morning we had these cattle penned, and at about two o'clock, the vet showed up and did the Broccolis testing (for Bangs disease) on a little over 225 head of cows.

Now, my brother Hershel was in charge of this job, and he believed in the way the old-timers worked: get there before day and stay till dark. I was thankful for the job, and I was getting a lot of hours on this young paint filly. The pay was fifty dollars a day and a cold soda water and a barbecue beef sandwich for dinner.

We had skipped a couple days of work when Hershel asked me if I wanted to help him hunt for stray cattle in a couple of big places joining this ranch. If we found anything and got it penned, I'd get a day's wage. If I had to rope anything, I'd be paid by the head; but if we didn't find nothing, then I wouldn't draw any wages. We hunted most of the day and found none of the four brands we were looking for. However, this is life, and it comes with the territory.

That coming Saturday, Mr. Bill Whiddon, who was the owner of the cattle on this ranch, wanted the entire pasture completely cleaned out of cattle. He was losing his lease on this ranch and had sold all of these cattle. Mr. Whiddon had brought in five more rope hands, but he upped the ante to fifty dollars a head on anything caught. It didn't make any difference what I thought about the deal. I'd worked three full days for fifty dollars a day, and I was figuring on getting my hands on some of that cheese, no matter whom he brought in. Two of the ropers were my nephews, Hershel Jr. and Judd Perry. When Judd said, "Unc, we ought to be able to make a month's wages here today," I smiled and said, "A month my foot! I intend on making out the rest of the year!"

Now, the upper end of this old ranch was mostly sandy fields, and in some places it was grown up thick, and in other places it was not so thick. We first went into an old field that had a good fence, with deep gullies dammed and made into ponds. The dogs bayed next to one of these deep gullies along the north fence line in a long, narrow thicket. I'd hung back with all those ropers out in the open field. I thought these cattle would come back up this fence line through the brush and cross over at the narrowest point, but what do I know? This black Brangus bull yearling went around this tank dam and across this open field. Those ropers managed to run over several dogs. I could hear Hershel stewing loud and clear. I was too far and out of the deal at the opposite end of this thicket and just waited. That black yearling outran those ropers and jumped into the fence and while tearing it down got across the fence. Judd was on the other side when he roped this yearling. I heard him holler, "I got mine, Unc! Get yours!"

I moved out into the opening still thinking that yearling had a mama and she'd have sense enough to come back that way. When they got the dogs started after this cow, she came my way; when she came out of the brush, I had a good angle on her, but this three-year-old filly hadn't ever lined out (run wide open). With an over and under with my rope, she liked to have run out from under my hat! We ate up the distance and were about to pass up this cow. As I tossed a big loop that went around this cow's head, I was trying to shut the mare down, and I missed picking up the slack in my rope. Finally, I grabbed the slack and managed to get all things shut down just as the cow went into the brush. I had managed to catch this yellow Brahman cow by one hind foot, and she was about twenty-five feet deep in the brush. (Now imagine that!)

The cow was doing some kicking, and this filly didn't understand what all was going on and was letting that cow pull us deeper into the brush. I got tired of that and got this filly turned around and headed back in the other direction to where we were able to see the opening. It wasn't long until I saw a group of those ropers coming. I took off my old hat and waved it back and forth from one side to another. The rest of those jug heads could see me sitting there waving my hat but couldn't see the cow and must have thought, *He's something from way out west.* They took their time getting to me. I let 'em know that there wasn't anything wrong with me that a truck and trailer couldn't fix. When they realized I had a cow caught, they all pitched in and helped get this cow out of the brush and loaded onto a trailer.

I had one other little incident that day. The dogs had a cow bayed that wanted to stay in this thicket and crawl around. Hershel got down afoot, but I'd stayed mounted and finally got her busted out of the worst part of this thick brush. I had my head down close beside this horse's neck and was running up on this cow. We were not close enough to get a shot (a loop). We kept running, but this cow popped out on this highline. I was thirty or forty feet behind her when out of nowhere these dudes swarmed down on me coming from the other direction and our horses ran together and hit each other. Now I was like the old-time cowboy that I heard about who thought, *He had the ride-a-way.* I'm sure glad that the rest of them pulled up, for I over and undered this mare as we caught up and noosed up my second cow.

At the close of the day, my filly was used up, and I was skinned up; but for the wear and tear, we both were in pretty good shape. Now, several of these old boys had 'em a nice ride. Judd was riding a blue horse that he and Hershel raised out of their horses that was one of the best all-round horses that I'd seen. Judd caught nine heads of these outlaw cattle, which made him a month's wage. But I was a little hungrier than Judd and had caught eleven heads of these cattle. I don't know why I didn't get my money when Mr. Whlddon paid Judd and the others. He asked if I needed any money, and I said, "Yes, sir." But Hershel spoke up and said, "If you're going to work Monday, let 'em pay you then." I was all for putting Monday's on today's pay when Hershel cut me a hard Perry look. I messed up when I said, "I'll wait." Now, I probably couldn't have gotten that check cashed, but it would've felt good just walking around with six hundred fifty dollars in my pocket instead of always being broke! But some things I don't guess are meant to be.

With a good feeding and a day's rest, Ol' Easter was shaping up to be a pretty nice using horse. I'd wished several times she'd been a little smoother balanced and had been a gelding. In the past, I thought you weren't mounted to do any heavy pulling if you weren't riding a big horse, and that's the way I had in mind of breeding my horses. But I changed my mind to less height, a lot wider between their front legs, and a better-balanced horse.

Monday morning, Hershel and me were sitting at the pens waiting on daylight and the rest of that crowd. Now me and Ol' Easter both could feel the effects of being ridden hard and put up wet. So I squalled a time or two as I stepped into leather, as this filly was learning to place her feet and come around pretty nice. We got the pen set up and had soon started drifting this bunch of cattle toward the pen. I was riding point on the right-hand side and had to lope up to swing a few head back into the middle that were trying to go wide when this misplaced farmhand let one of the cows that we had caught that Saturday beat him. No doubt she was salty and had leaving on her mind—taking all the dogs with her.

Mr. Whiddon hollered that he wanted her on that truck. I was a long way from the action, but when I saw Hershel pull a loop and swing wide, I swung wide enough to know when he turned her. We had position to throw her back toward the herd. But when he hollered, "Catch her," I didn't try making the effort to turn her hard, just enough to get a shot that fell pretty around those high horns. As I was slowing this filly down, the cow made a hard jerk.

Now, I really don't know; I guess this filly was sore. What I do know is when the cow put pressure on her, she ran forward and leaped high into the air. I remember losing my left stirrup as she hit the ground and the snatch that came behind that caused the mare to start jumping and bucking as I fell over her front shoulder. I must have fallen headfirst. Her feet hit me in the head. My head was the only thing fractured. I was knocked out long enough for them to call the justice of the peace and an ambulance.

As I came to, Hershel must have thought I wasn't going to make it. He had his back to the sun, was sitting on his heels with my head upon his knees, and was leaning over, saying, "Talk to me, Lloyd."

I opened my eyes and said, "What is it you want me to say?"

With a big smile he said, "Anything. You've been out over an hour."

I looked around and saw the ambulance and them getting out a stretcher. I said to one of the women there, "Ma'am, don't load me. I ain't got no insurance or any money." But I passed out again. When I came to this time, I was in the emergency room and said to the same woman, "Ma'am, why am I here?" She got to telling me stuff that I didn't want to hear, and I tried my best to get up when a couple of them put me down and gave me a shot against my will.

A couple of hours later, Hershel came and got me and took me to his house for a couple of days. I kept telling him I'd be all right down at my camp; I could curl up like a wolf and get better or die. But he thought I needed air-conditioning and that pampering business of someone doing for me.

The second day it hit me. "What about my money? What about that hospital bill?"

Hershel hung his head as he said, "The hospital bill was more than you made. Mr. Whiddon took care of the hospital bill for you."

I cut Hershel a hard eye and said, "I'm about tired of folk taking care of me against my will."

After all was said and done, I had made one hundred fifty dollars for three days' labor and five hundred fifty dollars for the eleven heads that I had caught, bringing the total to seven hundred dollars. The ambulance ride, emergency room, and doctor bills all came to over eight hundred dollars. They all got their pay, but I didn't get a dime out of the deal.

IMAGINE THAT

$\mathcal{O}$n September 2, 1954, I started my freshman year at Navasota High School. Back in those old days, school started the day after Labor Day weekend. School classes took up at 8:00 a.m. and let out at 4:00 p.m.

Dad had served on the Singleton school board after World War II while our country was in transition. Folks who lived in the country were moving to the city. The old pump station had been closed down, and because so many families had moved away, Singleton was left with a big school and few students. Dad told me each school district hired their own teachers, and with so few children left, the school district couldn't afford all the teachers it required. So Shiro and Singleton consolidated their districts, each keeping their school open, first through fifth grade; and together they bussed the junior high and high school students to Navasota.

We'd moved from Anderson back to Singleton in the summer of 1961 into Momma's new home. I now had to walk to Singleton to catch the school bus by 7:00 a.m. We'd usually make it to Navasota by seven forty-five. Mostly all the seniors sat around in front of the Navasota High School. Everyone else was in the back where the buses unloaded. There was a long canopy with benches on both sides all the way to the back door of the schoolhouse.

Now, I had a place picked out far away from that back door and all those folks, as far as I could get. You don't think about lonely or how long it's been until you start reliving your life's story and see where you've always tried meeting life alone. Nevertheless, I've always thought I was in good company by myself with my horse and dogs. I hated school and often thought of other things to do and places I ought to be. More often I thought of a three-year-old sorrel gelding I had a lot of trouble getting rode out (broke). He was bad to buck, nervous, bigger, and stronger than the other horses I'd rode out. His bad attitude caused him to wear my old saddle a lot and be left tied up. He was nervous and pawed the ground a lot. I had to get him into a corner and get his old head pulled around toward me while hurrying up to get into the leather at the same time just in order to get on him. I'd get his head pulled up as best as I could. Usually after the third or fourth jump, he would level out and ride pretty good.

School was a big interference. I held my spot for a couple of weeks when Jim Bay started coming over and visiting with me. He'd introduced me to an older, tall gal in blue jeans one day, right ahead of the bell. The next morning she showed up again. I wandered off and thought to myself that it might be about time for me to change ranges. The third morning when she showed up, I was getting up and fixing to leave when she called me by my whole name, but I didn't see how I could be in trouble. She asked, "Lloyd Perry, where are you going?"

"Ma'am, I don't rightly know, but I hope it ain't crazy."

"You know that's not what I'm talking about."

"Okay, then you never heard 'two's a party, three's a crowd'?"

"Please, sit back down and maybe I can explain."

I sat back down on the very end of the bench with my head down. She got up and said, "Look at me. I'm a long, tall country gal dressed in blue jeans and don't fit in with the girls of my senior class. I'm a cattleman's daughter and I'm sorry for pushing myself off on y'all, but I have no romantic interest in either of you. I just hoped I could be accepted and be among friends. I'm sorry that I took so much for granted."

She was fixing to walk when I said, "Why don't you sit down until we make up our minds?" She'd been sitting on the other side of Jim and made him move over and sit down between us. I smiled and said, "Hasn't anyone told you not to talk to strangers?"

She looked at Jim and said, "What's he talking about? I thought we were friends?"

Now, that girl was a real tomboy and was a very good friend until she graduated. We went to the Texas State Fair that following fall, and she had the time of her life, at my expense, seeing me nervously ride a Ferris wheel and roller coaster. Years later, I asked someone who knew her if they had seen or heard from her; they told me I wouldn't recognize her. "She's married, lives in the city, and wears a dress now." I said, "Imagine that!"

Lloyd Dowd
1-30-2001
Singleton, Tx.

LONG WAY TO WOODVILLE

Three retired schoolteachers and I made plans to go to a 42-domino tournament in Woodville, Texas. It started at about 10:00 a.m., and it was a little before 8:00 a.m. when these two retired lady schoolteachers pulled into my driveway. With a hot, stainless steel cup of black coffee, I had started to get into the backseat when this teacher got out saying, "No! No! You sit up here in the front and give directions."

I said, "No, ma'am," and started getting in. She then had a nice little teacher fit about it, so I got into the front seat.

Now, I'd decided those teachers are a different lot and it might take some getting used to. It's roughly seventy-five miles east of Singleton, Texas, to Woodville, Texas, and roughly seventy-five miles west of Singleton, Texas, to Snook, Texas, and that's where one of these schoolteachers was from. The one driving was from Bryan, Texas, and we picked up Mrs. Lowery in Bedias, Texas. All three retired schoolteachers, with one ignorant cowboy riding shotgun. Now imagine that!

We were thirty minutes into a two-hour drive, and they were visiting. I didn't have any comments of clever intellect to share in their conversation, so I laid my head back, pushed the back of my hat up over my eyes, and would've taken a nap if this lady doing the driving hadn't come down on me saying, "You're supposed to be sitting up here to help show me the way, not sleep."

I straightened up and said, "Yes, ma'am." The thought struck me again that these educators, who had been delegated authority, sure liked that authority. It must come with the territory.

Now, I'd played in a few tournaments against these lady teachers, but where we were going was close to the Alabama-Coushatta Indian reservation, and I was doubting that any of these old-timers ever played online for any mega bucks. The effect of civilization of these modern times hasn't had its way with everyone. It didn't make any difference about their age or if they were in a wheelchair or bowed over on a walking stick; they came to play, and they didn't mind beating on you like a drum, if they could.

We'd gotten past Huntsville, Texas, over to the east near Lake Livingston close to Onalaska, Texas, home of a friend of mine that I hadn't seen since I was a kid out of school, Mr. Willie Morrison, a good bullfighter and rodeo clown. I said to the lady driving, "Ol' Willie wouldn't take well with us speeding through his one-horse town." Well, I ain't for sure if this lady either had bad hearing or bad understanding. So I said, real plain, "We're in a speed zone, and you are speeding."

All that she said was, "I know that."

Now, we didn't go very much farther when these flashing lights came on behind us. She pulled the car over on the shoulder of the road, but I didn't understand why this officer came walking up to the car in the grass on my side. So I rolled the window down with a button and nodded my head in a cowboy fashion and said, "Morning."

He spoke and asked for her driver's license and was looking at me when he said, "Y'all was doing seventy miles per hour in a fifty miles per hour zone."

This teacher spoke up and said, "I'm sorry, officer, I didn't realize." Now, I cut her a hard eye as I took her driver's license and handed it to him. He had to go back to his car to run a check or something. While he was gone, she said, "Don't worry, I can handle this." But she'd never make me believe it.

When he came back up to my window, he had his thumb on her license on top of a book of tickets. When he looked at me, he said, "What's y'all's big hurry?"

I said, "It ain't worth telling, but we're late for a domino tournament."

"You all play?"

"Yes, sir."

"Where y'all playing?"

"Woodville, at the senior citizen center, I think. Maybe it's called a senior citizen pavilion or something like that."

He said, "I'm going to give you a warning ticket. See that you slow down to the speed limit." As he handed me her warning ticket, he added, "Slow your partner down in these speed zones."

I said, "Yes, sir, I'll do my best." I wanted to ask about ol' Willie, but for time's sake, I let it pass.

These other two ladies brought up that they had heard me say we were in a speed zone. Now, this lady from Snook was laying it on hard, hot, and heavy, and it seemed that I remembered some of them lectures from days gone by. I'd never seen a teacher get on another teacher like that! The Bryan teacher was driving but never spoke a word, kind of sulled up. I was feeling pretty good, her getting her education broadened, and this lady from Snook was making me look kind of like I was a hero, saying she ought to be thankful I brought up the domino tournament, for if I hadn't, he'd still be writing that ticket.

Now, this lecture and conversation went on for nearly an hour, and it looked like things were going to let up. Nobody said anything after a few minutes. I guess it was kind of bad, but I didn't want anyone to think I was a hero or that there was anything good about me. Matthew 19:17 (KJV) says, "And He said unto him, 'Why callest thou me good?' There is none good but one, that is, God; but if thou wilt enter into life, keep the commandments." Because I didn't think she ought to get off that easy, I reopened that can of worms. "Wonder if that officer is a domino player?" I didn't say any more, for here we go again!

Finally this lady driving said, "All right! All right! I'm driving the speed limit."

I smiled and said, "Experience and repetition are really good teachers. I've nearly got a PhD in doing it over and over until I'd got it right." The two ladies in the backseat laughed, but I could tell by the look in this teacher's eye that she thought I was riding a good horse to death.

After a long two-hour trip, we were in Tyler County, Dogwood capital of the world. As I stepped down on the ground a little before 10:00 a.m. in Woodville, I kind of blew out a little making a "Whee—ee-e" sound, knowing to give thanks. I then said, "It looked like one time we weren't going to make 'er."

This one lady in the backseat must have been enjoying this, for she said, "We could still have been waiting on the officer to finish writing up that high-priced ticket if it hadn't been for you!"

Now, I drew one of the natives from that country as a domino partner. We came a-smoking it! I don't know how well the lady schoolteachers did in the tournament, but this one doing the driving sure wanted to beat on me when we played them!

After my partner and I won the tournament, these schoolteachers and I got started back home. I was keeping my mouth shut until we got back to Lake Livingston when all I said was, "Wonder if we got time to stop in Onalaska? I'd like to see ol' Willie." The look I got told me to jump in the lake. So I smiled and said, "I'll catch him another time."

I'd always heard when the female gender got flustered and mad about nothing that they weren't mad but they really liked you. Now, I'd never known but a couple like this, and I was pretty sure that theory was wrong about one of them; the other one, well now, I couldn't figure her and was too chicken to try.

This had been a well-kept secret until now, but I had these two tickets to see Baxter Black, a cowboy poet, at Reed's Arena in College Station, Texas. Driving over there in traffic is about like driving in Houston, Texas, and I don't fare well when I don't know where I'm going. So I rung this old gal's number and said that I had two tickets to see Baxter Black. "Now are you interested?" When she said, "Delighted!" I said, real low to myself, "Imagine that."

OL' RACE HOSS

Along the whole north wall and part of the east wall of my log cabin, I'd built cabinets, and upon top of these cabinets were around sixty heads of good hog skulls with long cutters, from one and a half to two inches long. They wouldn't impress no one but an ignorant cowboy, and especially a young cowboy. I call these hog skulls, pictures that I drew, and domino trophies "trinkets" that ain't worth nothing. But that's about all I got to show for the three years that God took to show me these hard-to-see sins in my life.

I was sporting an attitude while living on the edge along about this time in my life. I don't recommend it either, for it's crazy and could get you killed. Now, all these old skulls have a story, but I can't take credit for Ol' Race Hoss's skull, for I didn't get 'em. Fact is, he run out from under my dogs every time I ran him, and unto this day I have no idea where this hog went, other than it was a far piece.

I found where he'd crossed the Old Bundy Road and once where the Navasota River forks and it surrounds Cane Island, an old outlaw hideout. There was a hog track and dog's tracks still going south toward Highway 21. I'd been stopping at Cane Island because I didn't want trouble with anyone. Hearsay was that two different sets of hog hunters were threatened to be filed on for trespassing by two different landowners. In one of the deals I know the old boy that had just caught a hog and had the hog laid on its side, one knee on the hog's neck and the other knee somewhere on the side of the hog. This old boy had the hog by the front foot and was fixing to tie it down when a woman and a man came upon him. The man had the gun; the woman was hollering, "Shoot him! Shoot him!" The man had the gun on this old boy until he'd gotten within a few feet from him. The man looked like he was taking his gun off this old boy when he shot the hog in the head within inches of this old boy's leg. When the woman saw that he'd killed the hog and not this old boy, she said she wanted the gun and was cussing them both. The man said, "Don't come back." Now you can see why I stopped.

Now, I never heard my dog, but if I had, my crazy mind was made up. I thought if you live by the gun, then you'll die by the gun. If you don't die, you're in a heap of trouble, and jail ain't no good place to be. I keep telling myself, *Don't put yourself in that position.*

I talked to my brother Hershel about this hog, for our hunting territory overlapped. Hershel and his boys were good hog hunters, and I enjoyed our hunts together. But Hershel liked to hunt with several people, and I didn't like to be around folks. When I told him about this old hog, I learned that Hershel had also run him without any success. It was just before deer season. Mr. Howard Slone, Hersh Jr., Hershel, and myself had us a plan to try and surround him. We found Ol' Race Hoss in some cutover country where he'd stayed. Soon as we heard a dog bark, we tailgated the rest and had him cut off from the way he'd go to the river and then run south. He came close to us but turned, and went north back to Cain Creek, and then to the river and on south. We coursed, followed, and trailed the dogs, because tracking collars were relatively new and expensive.

He went out of hearing distance to the south, and we followed six miles down the river. They went back for the trucks and were going to try listening off Highway 21 to see if he'd crossed it then come around the other side of the river and listen. We were all to meet back at Bundy Crossing by dark.

Having found a big downed tree across the river into Cane Island, I didn't find any dogs or outlaws, but I was watching for a hellion woman. My young dog, Lou I, and one of Hershel's dogs came to me as I was blowing my goat horn. I had about an hour of light and thought about a big rattlesnake I'd seen near Twin Lakes while day-working cattle and decided to light a shuck for Bundy Crossing before it got dark. We'd gathered four of our dogs before leaving that night. Old Queen (my dog) and another dog were back where we had turned out that next morning. Everything but Hersh Jr.'s old Roscoe dog was in, whom we searched for two days following. When Ol' Roscoe had almost made it thirty miles toward home, Joe Briers recognized him and took him to Hersh's home in Anderson, Texas.

Now, Bill Bay knew this hog had put it on me several times. Bill has the Twin Lake Ranch leased for cattle and for deer hunting. He was deer hunting one evening when Ol' Race Hoss came from the south, going north. Bill made a long shot across an open field, killed that old hog, loaded him, and brought him to me. Though I'd never seen this old hog before, I said, "That's Ol' Race Hoss. A tall, lanky boar hog that I'd run a dozen times but had never seen or ever known where he went."

OL' BUNT
MY SECOND EXCEPTIONALLY GOOD TOP DOG

*I*n the old days, what a lot of men lacked in the ability to cowboy up, they'd try to make up the difference in having a good dog. Now, from the time I was a little kid, I was always a sucker for listening to old-timers tell stories about something funny that happened to them. While listening to these old-timers, some would make mention to a certain old dog by name, and some of 'em would express how fortunate a man was to have owned an exceptionally good top dog.

Dad and I were alone when I asked him, "Why do these men say that they're fortunate just to have owned a good dog?"

Dad said, "Son, that's their brag dog. If you keep raising dogs, you'll know it if you ever have one. And chances are nothing else will come close to ever being like that dog in all the rest of your life."

Several years later in the fall of 1967, I'd turned twenty-four years old. Ol' Blue whelped one puppy that I called Ol' Mitzie. She was a dark blue gyp that was a one-man dog, who left her mark on me as an exceptionally good top cow dog, an exceptionally good hog dog, and a good top tree dog. I'd never owned a dog that excelled like this gyp.

Now, I never told anyone of all the hours in a saddle that I spent thinking of how I intended to breed and raise my own string of dogs out of my dad's bloodline of dogs. I planned to use Ol' Mitzie and Ol' Jr. as my foundation stock. Ninety-nine percent of these puppies were black, 2 percent were one-man dogs, and 20 percent were top dogs. But not a one of them excelled above Ol' Mitzie. I was inclined to begin to agree with these old-timers that an exceptionally good top dog must be a freak, for it had nothing to do with breeding and training in some respect. But whatever it was, I couldn't reproduce it or make it happen. Strange how some of my dogs liked a cow and wouldn't bay a hog or liked a hog and wouldn't bay a cow. I had a top cow dog gyp I called Mitzie II that I sold to Mr. Bill Wells of Singleton, Texas, in 1992 that won outstanding dog in the Gulf Coast Cow Dog Field Trials. Mitzie II wouldn't bay a hog but was an extremely good cow dog.

I was forty-eight years old when I made it back to Texas in 1993. I was going through the worst crisis of my life. My brother Hershel gave me a puppy, which I called Lou I, out of his gyp, Ol' Dixie. I considered Ol' Dixie the best hog dog I ever went in the woods with. Ol' Dixie was a black gyp that was a granddaughter of a dog that I had raised and called Ol' Cowboy. In 1993, when I returned to Texas, Hershel gave me the pick of the litter of nine puppies, which I called Ol' Lou I. I bred Ol' Lou I to Mr. Curtis Luthie's dog called Ol' Louis, who was of the same stock of my string of dogs in his bloodline. It was out of this litter of puppies that Ol' Bunt was born, a gyp that was as black as three foot up a stove pipe that made my second exceptionally good top dog on both cattle and hogs. Six months later, Luther gave me a pup out of his Ol' Rose gyp that I called Katey.

It was these three dogs (Lou, Bunt, and Katey) that I couldn't get stopped off of a hog one cold winter day in 1996. That was the day God brought me to the end of myself, as He delivered me and my dogs out of a critical situation. Now, as I was getting out of that country, I'd said several times, "Thank you, LORD." After foot-backing it over a mile, I stopped to rest and give God thanks. As I was praying and thanking Him for hearing and answering my cry, saying, "LORD, how would you have me to serve you?" this verse of Scripture came to mind: "Whether therefore ye eat, or drink, or whatsoever ye do, do all to the glory of God" (1 Cor-inthians 10:31, KJV). I then asked, "LORD, how do I do this in my line of work?" Inwardly I felt impressed to give God credit. I didn't realize when I said, "I'll do that," that that's against the carnal man (the flesh), for the flesh is against the Spirit of God that's sealed within one that's saved. It takes spiritual eyes to humble yourself in order to see that without Jesus you cannot do anything.

It was about a week later when Luther and I agreed to catch, sell, and split the money in half on whatever we caught each day. A killing plant in Divine, Texas, had upped the money on wild hogs, and for the rest of 1996, Luther and I hunted sometimes five days a week. We caught eight thousand dollars' worth of hogs in the year of 1996. It may not be a record, but it was a job catching 'em, tying 'em, going back, sometimes in the dark, and finding 'em, getting 'em to the trailer, and then marketing 'em, then getting home at 10:30 to 11:00 p.m., then feeding, eating, reading my Bible, going to bed, getting up about 5:00 a.m., and starting all over. (Now, life back here in the Old West don't get any better than that.)

But all good things end; in 1997 they broke the wild hog market in half. Luther went to doing more day work, either fencing or cattle, while I did the best I could at wolfing it. God allowed me enough day working to meet my expenses when Ol' Bunt begin to excel as a cow and hog dog in 1997.

I'd gotten through day working early enough to go check my cattle and a deer feeder one evening, and as I walked to this feeder, Ol' Bunt followed along with me. She began to smell and take on over this cold hog sign that was left at the feeder. She then left and was gone on this hog sign for over forty-five minutes. I had parked it under a tree and was sitting, waiting on her, when she bayed. I thought to myself, *Imagine that!* Now, I knew she had potential of being an extremely good top dog, but I wondered if she had that cold of nose or if it was by accident that she found this cold, laid-up hog.

I was in a cow-working crowd, and there were some hog tales being told. Ol' Bunt had found hogs late a couple more times. I decided I'd let it out and see if there were any challenges by the rest of these hands. I made this statement among several hands: "Anybody ought to be able to find a hog early in the morning. Most any dog could hot nose hog sign to its bed. A person ought to be able to do this with a Fice (small dog). But if you really want to know what you're feeding, wait and go hunting in the evening." Now that kind of talk put a hush on this crowd of cowboys. I wondered if they understood how cold that hog sign was that late in the afternoon. How unusual for a cur dog to be able to cold nose cold hog sign.

After dinner, we were waiting on the man in charge. I'd been sitting on my horse listening to this babbling about folks knowing who you are and what you are. I laughed when Luther told a tale about somebody asking him, "Boy! What do folks call you?" He said they all knew him as "Will Catch-a-Calf!" Now I had a smile on my face, for nobody knew me and Ol' Bunt as "Could-Find-a-Late-Hog."

So I then said, "Most folks will know you by what you ride and what's following you."

It was a month or so later when late one evening, about five thirty, Mr. James Ramsey, known as "Skeeter," pulled up to my house. I'd hollered for him to get down and come in. I noticed he had his horse in his trailer. I figured he'd made a day somewhere and had stopped to visit before going in.

He said, "Mr. Perry, what you got going on this evening?"

"Nothing."

"Got time to make a little round?"

I smiled and said, "Let me get some leather thrown on my bronc."

We could have ridden a half mile behind my house, but two old drag-around tied-up gates and a wire gap caused me to throw in with him, and we rode around to where I was wanting to go in his truck and trailer. We'd parked in an open pasture and had ridden toward Gum Creek since it runs west the same way we were riding. This was open country we were riding in, but with some scattered woods. But to the south there were woods and a real thicket known as the old Neece land. We got to a fence line that separated this bottom field from the old Neece thicket. We were riding up a fence line when we came upon a game trail that went under this fence. Ol' Bunt went to smelling on the wire, on weeds and bushes, with her taking on that way.

I just pulled my old pony up, slung my leg around the saddle horn, and said, "Let's wait and see what she does."

About then I was remembering Skeeter being in that crowd about a month before when I made the statement about folks knowing about what you was riding and what was following you. I was kind of figuring he'd might've come over to have a look-see at what I was feeding. Now, I was fifty-two years old, and he was barely eighteen, so I thought I'd check out his education and see if he'd done his math.

I said, "Do you know how many hours cold that sign may be?"

When he didn't say anything, I said, while looking at my watch, "If that hog came through here at daylight and put up (bed), that sign this time yesterday would be twenty four hours cold."

I don't think what I said was boring him any. I thought maybe he just hadn't figured up the hours. As a hand, I knew Skeeter had the potential of being a top hand, the same as Ol' Bunt being an extremely good top dog.

After Ol' Bunt had been gone twenty to twenty-five minutes and we were still sitting there, Skeeter asked, "Mr. Perry, how long does it usually take her to bay this late?"

I shook my head and said, "That I couldn't answer, for I don't know; but if Ol' Bunt don't find hogs, she'll come back to where she started from."

I didn't tell him how little my part was in this deal and that I was a confidence builder only. If she couldn't find hogs, she'd come back, for she had confidence that I'd be waiting. And if she found hogs, I would usually pat her on the head as a reward, but my biggest part in the deal was just trusting God and giving him credit and all the glory that he rightly deserved. About thirty minutes had passed when she bayed.

Now, Skeeter woke up Ol' Porky, this old sleeper (horse) that I was sitting on, with a loud squall, saying, "Now that's what I call a hog dog!" Then as he laughed, he said, "A Perry dog!"

Now, Skeeter may have not known that he spoke of a fifty-year dream of mine, and that humbled me. I realized God had laid Ol' Bunt into my hand as well as Ol' Porky as a tool to be used for God's glory.

I fell on some hard times in 1998 and had a chance to sell Ol' Bunt for $2500, thinking perhaps God would help me raise up another one, and he did. Lou II was the third exceptionally good top dog, but in 2002 she was accidentally shot. I then had a young gyp out of Lou II that I call CC Rider who also became an exceptionally good top dog that I thank God for. In 2004 a hog hooked (stuck) Ol' CC Rider in the back leg, which nerved a tendon, causing her foot to fold under her for over a year until God healed her by straightening out her foot. Ol' CC Rider was my fourth exceptionally good top dog and maybe the best dog that I ever owned. Ol' CC's mother, Ol' Lou II, was my third exceptionally good top dog. Ol' Lou II was a half-sister to Ol' Bunt, who was my second exceptionally good top dog. In 2008 God gave me another exceptional good top dog named Skittey, who died in 2009. Ol' Sue Baby is now the exceptionally good top dog.

Lloyd Perry
Singleton, Tx.

RANCH HAND RODEOS

In the early 1990s, I first began hearing about ranch rodeos. These rodeos were being held down in south Texas, and at that time I was living in Talihina, Oklahoma. Now, I had gotten acquainted with an old champion bulldogger, Mr. Don Huddleston, who was from Talihina; and in a casual conversation with him, I was telling him about the newfangled rodeos and that they had a lot of folks talking back in the Lone Star State.

It was only a few months later that we heard they were having a ranch rodeo in Durant, Oklahoma. So we went down into that old Red River country to have a look-see. Now, from the best that I could make of it, the stock was furnished by a local rancher, and the teams were made up of four men to a team. They didn't necessarily all have to be off the same ranch, but if they were, usually the ranch would sponsor them, as they rode for the brand. All the teams back then had a brand inscribed on a handkerchief and penned upon each cowboy's back.

Mr. Huddleston had some good facilities at the base of Buffalo Mountain. We held our first show that fall, along about the time the foliage was turning its different hues of greens and reds. The timing and the weather was good, and God's creation was a beautiful sight to behold.

In the ranch rodeo, we used some of Mr. Huddleston's old worn-out dogging steers in the mugging (roping and tying). I was still in the yearling business and furnished a small set of steers for the branding and a larger set for the penning. I also had a good set of Brangus cows on Mr. Jim Wade's place that we used in the wild cow milking. We had several teams show up with their families from three different states. Mr. Don Henderson and team came up from Texas.

The next year, that fall, Mr. Huddleston wanted to move up to the bigger rodeos and do the finals for the states of Arkansas and Oklahoma. My expenses went up, as I still furnished stock for so much a head, but I wasn't into big-timing it and graciously bowed out of being a ranch rodeo producer.

It had been several years since I'd quit the ranch rodeo business when an old friend, Mr. Sammy Richards, sent me word through the cowboy grapevine that he was going to try and make the Crockett Ranch Rodeo. Now, the motor had blown up in my ride, and I was down to a borrowed car that I called Old Helen. When Mr. Bill Bay asked if I'd like to catch a ride with him to this ranch rodeo, I enjoyed myself, seeing some of the locals compete. But something happened to Sammy's team, for they no-showed.

It was several years later when one day Mr. James Ramsey (Skeeter) and I were talking, and he was telling me of an upcoming ranch rodeo in Hamilton, Texas. Five men to a team, $800 entry fees, guarantee $50,000 for the first-place winners. Now, it seemed like to me this could be the granddaddy of 'em all, for it was to be shown on RFD TV, and a saddle was to be given to the top performance horse. I had heard something had been changed in the rules, about how the rider and horse weren't to get out of a walk behind the line while the rider went into the cattle. If he broke the rule, a full-time would be given. So Skeeter didn't ride his favorite mount (Ol' Bay) but borrowed a good mare from Mr. Curtis Luthey (Luther).

Luther called me Thursday night to see if I wanted to go to Hamilton to see this show that Friday evening. My schedule wasn't so pressing that it couldn't be altered, so he told me to be ready after dinner, and Mr. John Butaud would be picking me up. About 1:30 p.m., John picked me up, and while he was buying the car a tank of gas in Roans Prairie, Texas, he took some kind of contraption out of a box and mounted it up on the windshield. I had no idea of what this high-tech gadget might have been when he told me it was a GPS unit that he called "Susie." As we pulled out, "Susie" was talking and giving directions. I wasn't all that impressed with this high-tech toy until we got to Waco, Texas, and "Susie" went to spitting out highway numbers and telling John which lane to get into. With "Susie's" help we found Hamilton, Texas, and the Circle T arena, where we watched Skeeter and his team put on a roping clinic. I ain't for sure that "Susie" wasn't the most impressive, even if Skeeter's team did win the Friday night show. But I admit I was glad for all the boys on Skeeter's team when they came back the next night in the finals and won the show and the $50,000!

SADDLE TRAMP

Oftentimes inferior common labor has referred to a hand as a here today, gone tomorrow drifter or saddle tramp, mainly because things didn't go well and the hand rolled up. More than likely somebody in the crowd couldn't hold up their end of the deal, and they were allowed to stay within the crowd.

Whatever the reason, a cowboy won't go through the procedure of complaining or explaining things with no dude. He'll file it in chapter eleven and roll up. Being here today and gone tomorrow, because of principle, doesn't mean he won't work or that he's no good or that he won't ever amount to something. It's the other way around; a hand knows his work and does it well. His preference is being on horseback, but he knows there are other things he has to do, especially if he has a setup of his own.

Everyone lives by some code of ethics, good or bad. The unwritten code of the West is based on good morals, respect, and honor. If a cowboy draws some rancher's wages, he defends that ranch like it's his own. That's what is meant by "riding for the brand."

Every cowboy is known by his character, for that's who he really is. We honor or dishonor our own name as we build our reputation.

This is what's meant by "his word is his bond." A hand doesn't want to be roped into a crowd that's not right, for he knows if he takes their wages, he's committed himself to that brand. When he sees something against his principles, he won't compromise this honored principle. He'd rather be called a saddle tramp or all the names above than overlook what's not right.

I've always seen these kinds of saddle tramps as diamonds in the rough.

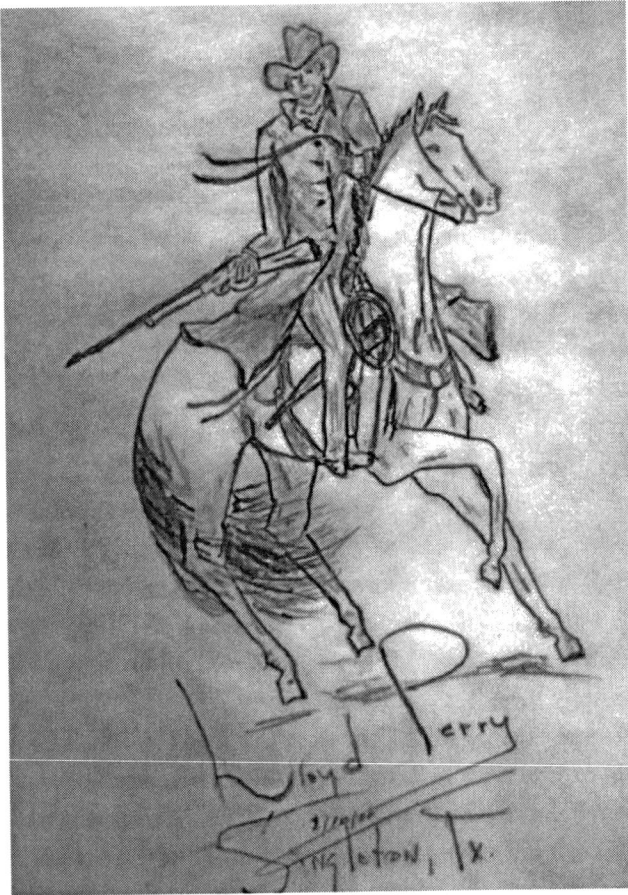

A HAND

*I*t's commonly accepted that among cowboys, they are known to be carefree. Often cowboys are called drifters. It has also been said that cowboys are unpredictable and often undependable.

It's not possible to speak for all professing cowboys; however, I will stand up for the professional cowboy, who is called by other cowboys "a hand." To be ascribed the title of a hand is a very high honor among cowboys. This title has been handed down through the years, dating back to the first great American cowboy.

- A hand has proven to have the ability and is known to have the respect of others.

- A hand would agree that his rights end when they infringe upon the rights of others.

- A hand doesn't fabricate the truth.

- A hand won't be roped into swinging a wide loop (stealing).

- A hand will live out the unwritten Code of the West.

- A hand's reputation will always precede him.

Therefore, it's very important to a hand that he protect his credibility and his character. Most often a hand would rather be self-employed and take cowboy wages than take common wages (paycheck). But sometimes things don't pan out, even for a hand. If he chooses to drift in search of employment, it's known that many before him have ridden a grub line in search of suitable work. When he does land a job, a hand will know in the course of a day's work if he's in the presence of other hands or just pilgrims. A hand expects of himself to do his part and more, but he refuses to be used by anyone who cannot hold up his end of the deal. It's not the way of a hand to be a downer. A hand doesn't share his grievances nor make any complaints. Yes, a hand is carefree, for he was looking for a job when he found this one. A hand would rather drift than to ride for a brand that is not on the ups.

CREAMY CHOCOLATE CHERRIES

$\mathcal{T}$he independent school district of Shiro and Singleton consolidated after World War II. Folks all around these parts were packing up and leaving the country. They all were going to the big cities in search of employment. Rural communities were all greatly affected by the vacating of so many people, especially small businesses, schools, and churches. These two communities sought to hold their schools open for grades first through fifth and join together in the expense of bussing their junior high and high school students to a larger district some twenty miles away to Navasota, Texas.

It was over a mile from where we lived to the schoolhouse in Singleton. In warm weather, my older sisters and I would get up early and walk to catch the bus. My sisters caught the school bus at 7:15 a.m., where the county road that we lived on intersected with Highway 90. I had to walk another quarter of a mile to Singleton. In cold, rainy weather, Mom or Dad would take us in Dad's old three-fourth ton Ford truck. If it was raining in the evening, I had to wait at the store. Most of my life had been hurry up and wait on somebody else!

During this time there were three small businesses left in Singleton. Two sold groceries, hardware, and feed, and one of these had a gas pump. The third store sold material and dry goods and was also the post office. Singleton had a train depot at one time, and several people, including Dad, would buy feed by the train boxcar loads.

Mr. McGilberry's store was where I did most of my trading. I was given a nickel each day to buy whatever I wanted for the trip home. I'd usually get a holiday sucker bar that I called a Slow Poke, for it would last nearly all the way home. I'd leave Mr. McGilberry's store, head down Highway 90, take a shortcut through the pump station, and come out on our home road at the cemetery.

One day as I went into Mr. McGilberry's store, I noticed six new boxes of creamy chocolate cherries in the candy case. I'd been watching and counting those boxes every day. I'd told Mom about 'em, and when one box was missing, I'd ask if Mom or Dad had bought a box yet. Mom liked these creamy chocolate cherries, and they would have been one of my favorites too if I could have ever had more than just one. If I asked for another one, Mom would answer a sharp, "No!" I knew better than to say anything else, for it didn't take much for Mom to set your timing up if you pushed her envelope.

It was the last day of school before our two-week Christmas vacation, and I was needing a break! I got to the store a little after 4:00 p.m. and noticed there was only one box of those creamy chocolate cherries left. When I asked if Mom or Dad had bought a box, the lady answered, "No." Mr. McGilberry had heard our conversation and must have known how I would have enjoyed eating more than just one of those creamy chocolate cherries.

When he said, "Erma, it's Christmas; give Lloyd that box of creamy chocolate cherries," she just stood there looking at him like it hurt her to obey him.

I thanked him and wished him a Merry Christmas. I began to get all kinds of instructions from Mrs. Erma on how many to eat. I didn't understand then why I had to make all those promises when she didn't want to give them to me no how. I was being forced to tell a lie in order to get my box of candy, and I didn't like it. I lit a shuck out of there, took the shortcut through the old pump station, and got ahead of my sisters. For someone who hated to walk as bad as I did, that was the most enjoyable walk home that I ever remembered. All the way home I was popping those creamy chocolate cherries in my mouth like a chicken pecking corn!

I was nearly in sight of the house when I threw that empty box away. I can say that at least one time in my life, I had my fill of those creamy chocolate cherries!

I have never wanted another creamy chocolate cherry ever again, not even unto this day. I was one sick pup that night and thought I was going to die!

HOG SCRAPE

I was classified as a freshman in high school and wasn't taking too well with the idea of doing four more years of time.

So I said to my dad, "They don't teach what I'm needing to learn in no classroom." I asked Mom and Dad to let me quit school and go to working on my own setup.

All Dad said was, "Nope, you can't quit till you graduate."

Well, I thought in time I'd get the point across, and having turned in blank sheets of paper all year, I failed everything but Agriculture 1 that year and drew a lot of flies and horse pictures!

During that summer I'd ridden several colts for the Polk ranch that my brother Hershel worked for. I had worked out a good Brangus heifer that I called Clara Ann, after the boss's pretty daughter.

When Hershel brought me what he said was my final paycheck, he said, "Keep enough to buy your school supplies."

I said, "That ain't necessary, for I ain't going back to school."

I noticed he hesitated before saying, "I believe you'll go." He saw that I was tied to a dream, and he knew my way.

After I got home, I told Dad, "I didn't fare so well in school. I only got one and a half credits and need fourteen and a half more before graduating. I didn't find nothing about school that ever helped me in my life."

Dad said, "You ever think about joining the army?"

I said, "Ain't ever crossed my mind." But I was going to call his bluff and said, "That ain't what I want to do with my life."

He said, "I know that. It'll take you five years instead of four to get out of school."

I walked away mad. It occurred to me I had the option of leaving home or going to school. We called it *our* home, but I didn't call what was my dad's mine or ours. Dad's old dogs wouldn't follow me or nobody else but Dad—they were his dogs. Now, he'd given me my start, and I was to have a dog of my own. He might buy the feed, but I did the training and whatever work it took to own it. My dad and mom had a bond between them called a vow. They took it in God's presence, and it didn't seem to separate them. They loved me and wanted me to prosper, but they didn't compromise, and neither will I. If you don't stand for something, you'll fall for anything. Dad didn't fall for my deal, and I was at a crossroads in my life. I either had to choose to abide or throw it all away. You can't hurt them that don't love you. You will hurt only yourself. To hurt them that do love you, now, that takes guts to turn your back on 'em. That makes about as much sense as the fool who cut off his nose in spite of his face.

I started back to school, and the first thing I took was a bad whooping. I'd never been anywhere to any dances or seen any fights, but I thought I knew how it'd go. That whipping made me even more capricious. I'd made up my mind to cut everybody plenty slack, no PE, no study hall. All the rest of the time my nose was in a book. I was going to get those fourteen and a half credits in three years or die trying! I made it through that year and gained five credits. There's a difference in doing good and trying to get out of a bad deal.

I summered on a couple of young horses that I'd broke, of which one could buck away. I had a good breaking saddle and could get him rode most of the time. You had to ride this horse hard in order to keep him rode down, or he could flat buck away.

Now, school had started again, and I missed having someone to talk to. When this dark-eyed, black-haired maiden opened a conversation on the school bus, I sat up straight and started doing a lot more talking than usual. I never knew what caused me to get the cold shoulder; however, days passed, then weeks, and she didn't have nothing more to say. I'd gone back to looking out the window of that school bus when one evening she opened and closed the conversation shortly with, "Are they looking for you?" I had no idea why the deputy sheriff stopped the school bus and didn't believe it when he asked if I was on there. This gal looked at me as if she started to say something else then thought the better of it. She turned her head away, giving me the cold treatment of which I'd become used to. Coyote-ish like, I was cornered, with no place to run.

Everybody was asking, "What'd you do?"

I stood up and said, "Mister, I don't know why you're looking for me. I ain't done nothing wrong." I guess I felt it, even if I didn't hear it, but I knew that she didn't believe in me neither.

So as I walked the aisle and out the school bus door, the bus driver said, "I'll tell your daddy that they got you."

I try hard to never be disrespectful with words, for that's the cowboy way. Instead I had a hard look upon my face that could kill crabgrass down to the third joint.

That deputy didn't handcuff me but stayed close by so I couldn't run. When he put me in the backseat of his patrol car, I recognized the man in the front seat and asked, "What's going on?"

He said, "The sheriff wants to ask you some questions."

I said, "Stop by the house and let's get my dad."

The deputy answered, "That won't be necessary."

From then on I didn't know the number of that amendment, but I wasn't making conversation with folks that were railroading me. So I didn't answer any questions or make any conversation. When we got to Bedias, Texas, to Sheriff Ike Mize's house, he invited us in and to sit down.

Then he said to me, "Tell me what you know about the hog scrape."

I said, "Sheriff, I ain't got a clue as to what you're talking about."

The fellow I knew spoke up and said, "Didn't you tell it around that a cousin of yours caught a good hog on the Navasota River and had it in his pen?"

Now, them old men didn't like it when I showed a big smile and said, "Yes, sir, I did say that, but a good hog to me ain't necessarily a good-blooded hog like you're thinking. The hog I seen was solid black, cold-blooded, with long tusks about one and a half to two inches long, weighed maybe 165 pounds, not a mark on him, and wilder than a March hare." The hog that I was talking about was a wild hog and not someone's slop hog.

Sheriff Mize stood up and told the deputy, "Take him home."

Now, when the deputy got me to the house, it just happened Dad was sitting outside in an old metal lawn chair in the shade of a walnut tree by the butane tank. He'd gotten up and had walked out toward the deputy's side of the car. As I got out of the car, he told me to go on in the house. All this was out of the norm, for Dad was an easygoing man and I heard them all speak by first name.

As I stopped inside the door, I heard Dad say, "Dick, if you ever have a problem with that boy, see me first. Don't you be stupid and take him off that bus again. Understand?"

The deputy must not have understood, for Dad said, "Did I make myself clear?"

I heard him say, "Yes."

Then Dad said to the other fellow, "What's going on?"

The man answered, "It's all been a mistake, Jack."

Dad said, "Now, if you ever pull another stunt like this, I'm going to take it personal. Now, good day to the both of you."

Dad was easygoing, but I'd never seen him on the prod before. My dad was a diamond in the rough and had handled the situation about like he'd been there. That bus driver had left my books, and I was getting with all this homework when Dad came into the house.

He stopped and was looking at me as he said, "I stood up for you out there; don't ever cause me to stand in the wrong." I nodded my head in cowboy fashion and never said a word as he turned and never said a word more about it either.

Just for the record, I had my share of trouble with English I, II, and III. Not only that, during my junior year, Navasota I.S.D. changed the credit system from sixteen credits to eighteen credits in order to graduate. I checked around and found out Iola I.S.D. still graduated with sixteen credits. I lacked four and a half credits (the last half of English II and all of English III). I told Mom and Dad my dilemma. Mom transferred me to Iola I.S.D., and I finished school in twelve years with sixteen credits. I know that ain't exceptionally good, but for an ignorant cowboy, it ain't bad either.

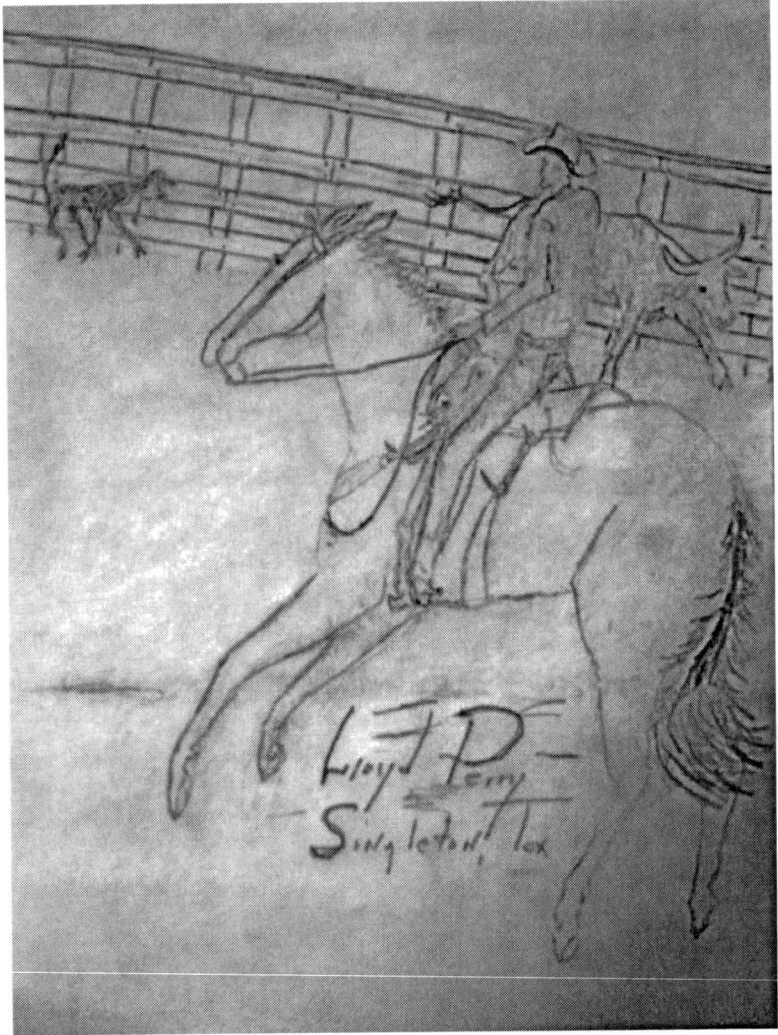

Floyd Perry
Singleton, Tex

SPECIAL COW SALE

The sport of predator calling of wild animals had greatly increased since that first time I'd gone with Mr. Moon, the old government wolf trapper and part Indian cowboy that I'd gotten acquainted with. Mr. Moon knew the secret of making good cowboy coffee: don't use much water.

It was nearly two years later that four of us got together to go calling at Russell and John Butaud's ranch. We were out for the Christmas holiday, just waiting for it to get dark while drinking coffee and visiting. It was brought up in a conversation that Mr. F.B. Moore of Huntsville, Texas, had put on a special stocker cow sale that past fall. The cattle had sold extremely high; a day hand could earn sixty dollars for two days' work. I was seventeen, hoping to graduate that next May and own a new truck and trailer. Therefore, I could see where I needed some steady employment and asked a few questions. I'd never heard of a special cow sale before and found out that Mr. Moore planned to have another one in the spring.

That spring I'd finally graduated and was now sporting a new 1963 Chevrolet truck and a sixteen-foot gooseneck Ed Hanover trailer. I made it over to the Huntsville Sale Barn early but wasn't to clock in until noon. Nobody was around the sale barn, so I moseyed on down to the Old Texan Café, where all the cowboys and cattlemen hung out.

Now, there is a cowboy grapevine whereby you are known by reputation. I looked around, and sure enough I recognized Mr. Buster Moore, an old-time cowboy, better known as One Loop Moore. He and Mr. F.B. Moore were no kin. Mr. Buster Moore was drinking coffee and nodded his head in cowboy fashion when our eyes met. I nodded back, for I'd never been introduced to Mr. Moore. I only knew he rode some good horses and had been a pick-up man at a few rodeos that I had attended. His son, Larry Joe Moore, also competed in the rough stock events and often picked up with his dad. Mr. Buster came over, and we introduced ourselves and had a lengthy visit.

I made my way back to the sale barn and found some of Mr. F.B. Moore's regular hands that were fixing to start pairing up some cows and calves. A barn secretary had arrived and took my name and started me on the clock. After getting signed up, me and another dude found these old boys waiting around in the back. Quite naturally, with their seniority, they had all picked their spots. They ran three or four calves in this pen with about thirty-five cows. The two new men were assigned the job to go in and to pair them up and then drive them out on foot. It wasn't bad if you say it real quick, for it was just that simple. You had better know how to make that move and be ready to stick fight a wild cow when it came time by holding your ground and forcing her and the calf to take the gate instead of peeling back into the bunch.

It didn't make any difference if the cow came out of East Texas piney woods or the swamplands of Florida. Those King-horned Brahman crossed cows would blow snot all over you while trying to hook you out of the way instead of going on up the fence line and on out the gate. It made a hand feel good to sort out a pair. He felt as if he had accomplished a mission. It took over an hour to pair this pen of cattle. I figured if all our work was to be like this, we were going to earn our wages.

As I was walking out of the pen, I passed the gate man and said, "I feed a horse to do this kind of work."

"Yeah, we do too, but it's good to see what a new man is made of."

"Really? How about a couple of y'all showing a new man how this is done?"

He replied, "We will."

I only smiled and kept all the rest of my comments to myself. I knew if you couldn't cut the mustard, you would most likely be sent packing it to the house.

It wasn't but a little while before we started another pen. True to his word, two of them started pairing. I'm for giving credit where credit is due. Mr. Cecil Smith was as good of a sale barn man as I ever knew. He was a ring man deluxe who could flat whack with a stick. Although I was young, I did my job and said nothing else.

We stopped and had a bite to eat about midafternoon after we had finished pairing. The owner, Mr. F.B. Moore, showed up, and one of the sale hands brought him a little sorrel stud horse. As we pushed about thirty to forty head of cows into the alley, under the barn, Mr. Moore would go in and cut a cow off. He had a center gate man and four men catching two ways each as he would call our name and direction as either left or right. I was highly impressed with the little horse, and by the time we got them all shaped, I knew I was working for a horseman and a cowman.

That night we unloaded a few trucks and trailers and a couple of big cattle trucks. I didn't get a chance to get any rest. I was tired, but there was so much noise, and I couldn't sleep slumped in a chair.

The next day I made the sale all right. I was assigned a job to bring up cattle. That was very unusual, being just a new kid. After the sale was over, we went to loading trucks and trailers then several big cattle trucks on up into the night. We finally did get a break, and my "dawgs" were killing me. The first chair I came to I flopped down on and got a thirty-minute nap. Then along about 2:00 a.m. a big truck came in and messed that up. I was rat ready for noonday to hurry up and get here. I was looking forward to sundown and payday. I got $62.50 that noon and went home and after a hot bath straight on to bed and didn't stir until late the next morning. After the special cow sale, I was fortunate to land a job on Tuesdays working at the regular sale, working for Mr. F.B. Moore.

It was only fourteen years later that I was peddling some high-dollar Moorman feed, when Mr. F.B. Moore bought a twenty-two-ton trailer truckload of Moorman Mintrate blocks. It was the first truckload and the largest amount I had ever sold one individual. I am appreciative of the friendship along life's way.

If it is the LORD's will, I hope to return the favor.

SWEETIE

$\mathscr{B}$ack in the nineties there were several old-timers around that enjoyed the game of dominoes. There were some who would play most any time; however, there were three of us—Mrs. Doris Lowery, Bro. Copeland, and myself—who would play any time we could get a game up.

We started out playing at Mrs. Doris Lowery's house, and that became our main base of operation. But we played at a lot of other players' homes also. Brother Clyde Copeland would bring our devotional before we began playing. I've always hunted hogs and would bring a package of homemade wild hog sausage that I'd cooked on a pit. We'd stop for a word of prayer, eat a wrap-around with several cups of coffee to wash down the spicy sausage, and put out the fire.

I was usually the youngest player at these gatherings. I began to just take it upon myself to get up and reheat or refill everyone's cup that needed coffee. We'd been playing for a couple of years when one night I got up and reheated or refilled everyone's coffee cup. A lady from over at the Methodist church was playing with us.

When I reheated her coffee, she said, "Thank you, sweetie!"

Then everyone laughed, except me. I didn't take too well to

being called "sweetie." I couldn't believe that even Brother Cope thought it was funny. Now there ain't no one, not even my own mother, ever called me "sweetie."

So in a low tone of voice, I said, "You're welcome, ma'am. But when I go to beating on you with these dominoes, you're going to be taking back that 'sweetie' part."

SWEET

*I*t was in September of 2008 that Hurricane Ike hit the Texas Gulf Coast. It turned and went east of Singleton, Texas; however, we had high wind and rains all day Saturday. The following Monday evening I went to check on my cattle, for I had been buying bred cows and had been holding them in a trap. I'd decided to put these cattle in my pasture the Friday before the storm on Saturday. This was the first chance I'd gotten to go check on these cattle. If any were gone, I was fixing to have some riding to do.

I'd gotten to within a mile of my place when I came upon a new car parked in the middle of the road. There was no one in the car, and a dead tree had fallen across the road. I was throwing limbs out of the way when I noticed four people walking back up the road. When they finally got to where I was, we spoke and were past our howdies.

In broken English one man asked me, "Is it far to Kellem Springs?"

I came back with, "That depends on if you're walking or riding. About a mile and a half."

The man said, "Oh! Mile and a half, I see, a longer walk than ride."

I smiled and said, "If you move your car, I've got a chain and will try to jerk this tree around so we can get by. Then maybe you can ride there."

"Maybe so, but there is another bigger tree about a mile from here."

"Let's see if we can get by this one. Then we'll look at the next one when we get to it."

We got by the first tree, but the second one was too big to move. I told them that I could go through my brother's place, for I needed to check on my cattle. As I was fixing to leave, they were thanking me for helping them get this far.

I said, "I'm afraid I haven't been much help. It's a long half mile to Kellem Springs, and you'll have to hurry to be there and back before dark."

The English-speaking man said, "We have tried."

They had gotten to America two days before the storm and had gone to Austin, Texas, to get out of its path. This was the first chance they had to come to Kellem Springs. The older lady was a professor and as a young lady had written some kind of paper or thesis about her many times great-grandfather, who was buried there at Kellem Springs. She said that she'd come a long way and had gotten close but that she would have to reschedule another visit to America. She had a map of where her many times great-grandfather was buried. The map showed his grave to be two hundred yards north of the house on a little hill. They had made this one walk to the tree and back to the car. They would have to reschedule, for their plane left the next morning.

I asked, "How come she needs to see this fellow's grave?"

The English-speaking woman said, "For the book." She called the professor's name and said, "She wrote a book about him." And she called this fellow's name.

I said, "In a case like that, it would take a miracle, but maybe

I can help. The pasture is wet, the creek crossing could be washed out, and the county road is slick and muddy with a couple of bad places. LORD's will, we'll try."

As I was cleaning out the backseat of my truck, I found a promotional poster of my book, saying, "Now available: *A Lasting Impression.*" I handed it to the English-speaking lady, and I suppose she read it but didn't understand it.

I said, "I'm a cowboy, not a book writer, but I was given the privilege of writing a book. I too had a professor to write in my book."

Now, that excited this English-speaking lady. She went to trying to translate American cowboy into French. The professor wasn't saying much, other than "*Oui!*" This professor was having the English-speaking lady ask me questions and then translate. I wasn't sure she got the dialogue right, for every now and then she'd hum like she might have been searching for a word to describe what I had said. That tickled me, for I guess they hadn't run into many uneducated cowboys in their circles that spoke something besides English (Texas cowboy slang).

They all finally piled into my two-seated Toyota truck. It was wet, so I kept up a good bit of speed and made it to the creek crossing. Those two women were going, "O-o-h!" as I eased off the north bank. About five feet from the water, I gunned it to have more speed going up the opposite bank. When I hit that water, both those old gals said, "Ah-ah-ah!"

When we got across and up on the south bank, the English-speaking lady said, "We made it!"

I grunted at that and said, "Not yet, but we're closer."

Then I told them about the Old Springfield Road and showed 'em its remains. I told them that we'd crossed the creek where stage coaches had traveled on the Overland Stage Coach going from Anderson, Texas, to Springfield, Missouri. We made it through my place and onto the county road, which had some bad places in it. We drove all the way up to the old Kellem Springs house and stopped in front. The professor got her map as the two men took pictures. I was asked about a nut tree. They asked if we have trees that bear nuts. I said, "Yes, ma'am." They asked if I saw any close by. I said, "No, ma'am." We spread out and looked around, but no one found anything. Daylight was gone as I drove them back to the tree in the road where they had parked their car. I didn't think they wanted to make that ride back across the creek.

I said, "Looks like we made it all in one day." They thought it was a good ride—a lot better than the walk. They were all shaking my hand and thanking me for all the trouble. Then the professor had the English-speaking lady tell me she deeply appreciated my hospitality and how that I went out of my way to help strangers.

I hung my head down and said, "You're welcome, ma'am." I asked them not to leave until I made it back around.

When I made it back, they again were thanking me and wanted to write down the name of the book and the publisher and my address. They were going to write me and send me some pictures they had taken.

I ain't much on good-byes, so I said, "We may or may not meet again, and I'd like to know that I have one book in France. I'd like to give the professor a book, but it's at my house." I was without electricity at my house, so I lit a coal-oil lamp. The first thing they noticed were some of my old drawings, and they took pictures of them then the domino trophies. I laughed when I shined my flashlight on those old hog skulls hanging up on the wall and the women went, "Oh-o-o!" The men found my house most amusing and took pictures inside and outside. Now, I was impressed with a camera that would take a picture in the dark.

When I wrote the professor's name in the book and signed it, I had no idea that she would say, "Sweet!" and then kiss me on the cheek.

I shook my head and said, "No, ma'am, I'm not sweet."

The professor nodded her head and said, "Sweet!"

I thought to myself, *The woods are filling up when you start running into Frenchies, but that "sweet" and "sweetie" about does it!*

THE REAL DEAL

*N*ow, it's my belief that God wants to work through his church. All who have been born again make up the church. The church is not the building but rather God ruling in the hearts of his subjects.

Most often church visitation falls by the wayside when we refuse to leave our comfort zone, expecting God to accept what we chose for our own ministry and forgetting about the will of God.

Our church went through a program called "Experiencing God." In this study we were told always to join God in his activity, that we were not to create activity. I agree with this statement, and if you continue knocking on doors, you'll quickly learn God's activity is not only God at work preceding you but God at work on our behalf in getting it God's way. We're to go in the Spirit, we're to go in faith, and we're to go in love, to name a few of God's ways for us to go. I also believe that creating activity is missing God's mark. Acceptable and appropriate worship is God's way.

In our visitation, we were sent out in twos for two hours on Sunday afternoons. We were given a survey sheet that asked a few questions. The last question asked, "Do you think it is important for a person to understand how to have a personal relationship with God?" Now,

I believe this question deals with being born again and with disciple-ship in the Lordship of our lives unto Jesus Christ. After the survey we'd ask if we could share our testimony. I've often begun by saying, "We may come from many walks of life, but we're all saved the same way, and Jesus is the Way. 'I am the way, the truth, and life; no man cometh unto the Father, but by me'" (John 14:6, KJV).

Mrs. Helen Cole was my visitation partner, a prayer warrior and very meek lady. We faithfully visited for a couple of years together. One Sunday afternoon we came to a house where there were only a couple of teenage boys at home. While Mrs. Cole was doing the survey, I silently prayed again, asking God to help us be sensitive to the Spirit, for we were trusting that this was God's activity and that neither of us would fail God by not getting this his way.

After Mrs. Cole finished the survey, she asked these boys, "What's your activity been through the summer?"

The boy who lived there must have been an ignorant cowboy because he said, "Ma'am?"

She then asked, "What do you do in your spare time?"

This boy smiled and said, "We're bull riders."

Mrs. Cole smiled and said, "Mr. Perry here is an old bull rider."

Now, my old crazy cowboy way caused me to grin, showing all my missing teeth as I said, "And I got the evidence to prove it too!"

Immediately a serious thought struck my mind. I said, "But I'm here to tell you about the real deal, the LORD Jesus Christ."

I asked if I could share my testimony, and they both said, "Yes, sir." Having shared with them how I'd come to know Jesus as my personal Savior, I asked if anything like that ever happened in their life. This one boy said, "No."

I turned to the other boy, and he said, "Yes, sir, I'm a Christian."

I said, "Pray for your buddy then." As I turned back to the boy who said no, I said, "If you realize that you're lost, without Jesus, and if you're willing to accept what He has done for you, His death upon the cross as payment for your sin debt, then His spirit is at work drawing you. We only come to God when he draws. John 6:44 (KJV) says, 'No man can come to me except the Father which hath sent me draw him; and I will raise him up in the last day.'"

We then turned to Romans 10:9–13, and I had him read it. After we knelt down and prayed the sinner's prayer, I asked him, "Are you saved?"

He said, "Yes, sir."

"How do you know?"

"Because the Bible said so."

I said, "Friend, that's good enough for me. Salvation is the first step in following God's Word. Get into a Bible-teaching, believing church and become all God saved you to be." To see someone accept the LORD and profess Him as Savior is about as close to your own personal relationship with God as you will ever get.

We never saw either boy again, although we went back several times to visit.

One day I'd heard of a death of a rodeo cowboy from the Bedias community. I went to my visitation partner and asked if she knew anything about the young bull rider or heard anything about his death. It was confirmed that this was the same young cowboy. He'd made his profession public and was baptized. He had been active in a cowboy's church.

THE TENDER YEARS

I'd made it to Texas in 1945, and no doubt the times were plenty rough back then, but I'll always believe they were better then they are now in this twentieth century, for I'm not into all of these changes of these modern times. It could be that I'm the only one who feels that way, for I live my life a lot different than the rest of the natives of today. Money in the 1950s and sixties was in short supply back then, but a dollar was worth a dollar. Though most of the folks were poor, it seemed that everyone worked and had plenty to eat, for back then the government didn't cause people to depend on it. When someone was having a crisis situation, folks would help one another. The name of God was lifted up in reverent fear. Now, growing up I only knew two kinds of bums, hobos and tramps, and they'd even work for something to eat. Nearly everyone in our county raised a big family and a big garden, and they all did a lot of canning in the summertime. I was raised on beef and wild pork, for if you didn't have beef in the summer and pork in the winter, you weren't living; you were just existing.

Now, of all the hardships that I observed back then, the hardest one I encountered was seeing Mom and Dad struggle to meet the obligation of a yearly land payment to the Federal Land Bank. After having observed my parents' sacrifice and struggle for their family and to own land, I began making my plans while forked in a saddle on top of a good horse. I'd been stuck in school a long time before they ever turned me loose and would have gladly quit, but my parents wouldn't hear of it. So I tried failing everything my freshman year by turning in blank sheets of paper and drawings. When it came time for school the next fall, I tried talking my parents out of having to go back. I thought I had enough schooling and told them I had a plan, that I'd get me a rig, and then I'd begin leasing land and buying cattle until I'd gradually built my herd up. Half the cattle I would sell. That would pay for a small place so I could build my own setup (house, barns, corrals, etc.). Now, they both sat there and listened to my plan, but both thought I needed to get my education.

I wanted to be pig-headed about this until Dad put his foot down and said, "Either go to school or else get rid of what you've got and join the army." That hurt mighty bad from the two people that I loved most and who loved me, but I managed to get all my credits over the next three years. That may not be that unusual, but it was mighty difficult for me.

After finally making it through the rough part of schooling, I made contacts trying to locate lease pastures so I'd be able to work my plan for life. I finally managed to lease one hundred fifty acres of old, rough wood country with about forty acres of old, worn-out fields. The grass wasn't good enough to run cows and calves on, but it was a cheap lease pasture. Dad helped me go around the fence, for it was in bad shape, but we got it overhauled before I put ten one-year-old heifers in that old place. As these heifers began to spring (show a calf), I'd move 'em back home to a trap so we could see 'em three or four times a day. Now, it wasn't my plan, but I had to improvise until I got a pretty good place leased and could buy enough cattle to stock it.

That fall I didn't sell any of my calves when Dad sold most

of his. That October, Dad allowed me to break up forty acres of land. I bought five tons of fertilizer and two tons of oat seed, putting down two hundred fifty pounds of fertilizer and one hundred pounds of oat seed to the acre. I had worked about ten days getting all this farming done. I then went to Waller, Texas, to see an old farmer whom I was told had ear corn for sale. I bought six tons that I had ground and then weaned all twenty-five head of my calves that would have averaged 385 pounds each. These calves were worth about seventeen to twenty cents a pound back in 1963. Dad held back about the same number of calves that would have averaged two hundred fifty pounds at roughly fifteen cents a pound. Dad and I made two sixteen-foot feed troughs out of two-by-twelve boards three feet wide. We had a one hundred fifty-gallon concrete water trough. I hauled three barrels of water morning and night. Dad had bought a load of alfalfa hay for his cows. I fed these calves corn and alfalfa twice a day and had to go back to Waller, Texas, for another load of corn.

Now, I'd gotten acquainted with this old farmer; however, he asked me a lot of questions about my business that I didn't, at first, really want to discuss. But he was just making conversation, and his wife and old-maid daughter were extremely good cooks. They also liked to drink a lot of coffee. The more I got to know these folks, I learned that he really cared and was interested in a young cowboy's plan. I remember going over to this farmer's place one time after having been bucked off a bronc. Since I was stoved up a might, that ol' maid daughter nearly loaded that whole trailer load of corn for me. The more I think about it now, I probably should have cocked my hat for that ol' gal, even if she was twenty years older than me. They were some good folks and really treated a young cowboy all right. I bought corn from this old farmer for several years right up until his death.

I fed these calves corn all of the month of October and November of 1964. No one in our country at that time planted winter pasture. I got my calves moved to my oat patch after Thanksgiving, cutting back the feed to once a day. The oats did good, and the calves started doing good also, but the market didn't do anything until that February. I rode the market into the end of March and then sold out. I was hoping to average one hundred dollars a head straight across for my yearlings. My heifers averaged over one hundred dollars a head, and my steers averaged a little over one hundred twenty-five dollars a head.

One of the few compliments that my dad ever attributed to me, outside of saying, "He's different," was when he looked at the check and said, "Ain't ever sold cattle that high before," as he smiled at me. I had no way of knowing that I should have kicked myself for this. Later on, Dad did his very best to turn a pretty good cowboy into a farmer and rancher by planting three hundred acres of winter pasture every fall.

1940 AND 2009 BIG OIL
SCARE IN SINGLETON

As a little boy I personally knew Mr. Jeff Mandly and Mr. Charlie Smith. The story is one that I heard told several years later after their deaths.

There was a wildcat drilling rig that ran off a steam engine that hit a pocket of oil west of Singleton, Texas. That same day they hit oil, Mr. Jeff Mandley rode horseback around the community of Singleton, telling all the folks that oil had been struck in Singleton.

At that time the community of Singleton was probably at its peak, with a large congregation of people that went to the Singleton Baptist Church, a large schoolhouse with an auditorium, an oil refinery plant, a train depot station, post office, four different store businesses, a pulp wood yard, sawmill, and several farms and ranches.

Now, when Mr. Jeff rode up to Mr. Charlie Smith's place north of Singleton, Mr. Charlie was plowing some bumblebee cotton (cotton that grew eight inches tall on poor, sandy soil); he was running middle with a Georgia stock and mule.

When Mr. Jeff came riding up, he threw up a hand to speak

and said, "Charlie, have you heard that they struck oil west of Singleton?"

Mr. Charlie pulled the mule up and said, "Whoa." He drew the plow lines up over his head and dropped them, pulled out a clean white handkerchief, walked around behind the mule, and sat down on the Georgia stock. He took to wiping his face and said, "Now, Jeff, tell it to me again."

Mr. Jeff said, "They struck oil there on Mrs. Fisher's place."

Mr. Charlie said, "My, my, there'll never be another poor day."

Mr. Charlie was still sitting there when Mr. Jeff rode off. A little later he got up and unhooked the mule from the plow, pulled the harness off the mule, then hung all of the harness upon the handles of the plow. He turned the mule loose and walked off toward Singleton to see what he could find out. He never went back for the plow or the harness but let it sit there in the field until it finally rotted. The oil pocket never produced a well. Mr. Charlie sat around town for the rest of his life. He had a few cows, but other than that, he never hit another lick or did any work.

Once again in 2009, there was another oil scare west of Singleton. And for a few old-timers like Mr. Charlie Smith, or myself, we don't mind sitting around playing dominoes or loafing, for I'm not bad about doing no work either.

DON'T MONKEY WITH
A MONKEY'S MONKEY

*I*t seems like ages ago that coon hides would only bring around five dollars. Then in the 1970s they took a jump to around fifteen dollars for a hide that stretched twenty inches or more. I hadn't had a tree dog since I was in high school, yet I thought one of the three old dogs that I was feeding surely might fit that position. If at all possible I was going to see if they had any potential.

Now, I knew an old boy that had a good pair of Red Bone hounds that he'd pleasure hunted with for several years. When hides went up, I heard he'd bought a little half-cur gyp that was the best hide dog in the country. I didn't see anything wrong with going over and visiting him, being as hide season was over. As we visited, he told me how many coon hides he'd sold. He talked about the two hounds being all right, but the cur dog was responsible for treeing all the coons. He encouraged me to bring a dog and come go hunting with him.

The next week I'd eased over to his house to go hunting and have a look-see at his dogs. We left about dark and drove over to my cousin Grady Allen's place. I had brought only one dog, Ol' Mitzie, who was my main cow and hog dog; however, she'd never been out at night and just stayed close to me, not knowing what I was doing.

When his two hounds struck and began to open, I sent Ol' Mitzie, and she went to them but never opened. We waited a few minutes before the hounds started moving up this spring branch. In about fifteen minutes, his half-cur gyp treed almost a quarter of a mile ahead of these hounds. He never said nothing, just took off toward the dog that was treed. When we got there, Ol' Mitzie was sitting there at the tree but wasn't barking. I reached down and petted her on the head to let her know it was all right. The two hounds trailed on in and were now treeing also. Now I thought, *What a deal he doesn't know what's going on!*

We found this coon and had agreed that we'd tie up the dogs. I climbed up the tree and jumped the coon out. When I got back down, we'd turn the dogs loose and have us a jump race. The coon had been gone about five minutes when I got down out of that tree. We turned loose the hounds and then the cur dogs. We listened to the hounds about ten minutes before the two cur gyps treed. Ol' Mitzie barked some this time. We did the same thing again, and the hounds did the same thing. After we found the coon, to be sure he was there, I caught my gyp and said, "I've seen more than enough; I'm ready to go to the house."

He asked, "Is something wrong? The night is young."

"Hounds and cur dogs aren't a good mix. I don't enjoy seeing what's happening to the hounds."

He said that he enjoyed listening to the hounds, that the cur just made short work of it.

I said, "Really? You don't see nothing wrong with hunting like this?"

"It ain't as good as if they were all together, but what's that going to hurt?"

I said, "Maybe nothing," as I caught my dog and started for the truck.

"Wait a minute." He caught his dog and took after me. "I appreciate hearing what your thinking is."

"It doesn't matter."

"If you won't tell me, that's all right, but I'd appreciate it if you would."

I said, "Buddy, every cowboy that I ever knew that was a hand, they were horsemen and dog men, and they knew the basic, fundamental facts of what's right and wrong. You know that if these dogs were all together, that would be right. You know that the hounds can't run with the cur dog. You know that the hounds are going to open (bark) on a track the cur dogs don't. Surely if you don't know, you've heard some old-timers say that a dog is not supposed to open on a covered track (what another dog has covered). Anytime a dog barks and he doesn't have the lead or the track, he is out of whack. He's supposed to shut up and catch up. If the dog continues barking out of whack, this is called babbling, and it's only a matter of time until this babbler will mess up the whole pack."

He said, "You think the cur dog will mess up the hounds?"

"Exactly."

Now as a kid, I always climbed a lot of trees. So after my little episode in wanting to get me a tree dog, I took to climbing some hollow trees, shining my light down into the hollow. If Mr. Coon was home, I'd drop a firecracker down in there upon him. After ringing his ears, Mr. Coon would make for the hole in the top of the tree. It was a good idea to be out of his way, for he was coming out. I never could figure out if it was the firecracker or just waking him up in the daytime. But I must have jumped two dozen coons out of holler trees that month. They all would pull out and show Ol' Mitzie and my other dogs a lot of real estate. She'd finally tree 'em, and she was making quite a tree dog. I started night-hunting her, mostly by myself. Then one day this old boy showed up at my house.

We howdied and shook hands, and then he said, "You were right. Those hounds got to where they hated that cur. If she went one way, they would go another, for they wouldn't run a track with her. They wouldn't honor her if she treed. If the cur gyp went to the hounds after they were trailing a coon, they'd pick 'em a tree and tree. There wouldn't be nothing there. When the cur treed, the hounds wouldn't honor her."

I never said nothing and wondered why he came to tell me all this.

He said, "I brought my gyp if you want to make a little round."

"All right."

We hunted a couple more times together. It was getting on toward December, close to hide season. He showed up one Friday evening wanting to go hunting. He'd heard that hides were going to sell good and that anything that would stretch over twenty-two inches would be bringing upwards of twenty-five to thirty dollars each.

In the few times we'd hunted together—I'd never admitted it to anyone until now—his cur gyp had a notch on Ol' Mitzie. I figured out that his gyp could wind and locate a tree when conditions were just right from the back end of the truck. She was by far the best hide dog I'd ever been in the woods with.

Now, my old home range gets rough to the south. We have in our country what old-timers called a "stump-tail hill coon." Don't think these old scoundrel boogers won't lay you out a track, even with two silent, fast-running cur dogs after him. It was unusual for a coon to run thirty to forty-five minutes ahead of these dogs, but the credit goes to the coon. We finally looked at him, and I started toward my dog, Ol' Mitzie, to leash her. When I saw him pet his dog and then reach over and pet Ol' Mitzie on the head, I said, "Hey, watch it, buddy!"

"What's the matter? They done good."

"That is not the point. The point is we all have ways, and I believe that a dog that becomes anybody's dog winds up being nobody's dog."

He smiled and said, "She likes me."

"Just don't pet my dog. If you do, I'll make her bite you."

He hee-hawed about like a mule trying to eat a mouth full of briars and said, "You can't make her bite me!"

Now, that made me plenty mad, and I said, "I will if you ever monkey with my monkey again."

I called my dog and wanted to leave, but he said, "I don't believe that'll ever happen. Why don't you show me?"

Now, I was a young Christian and I failed God, for I cursed and told him, "Let it pass. Let's go."

He said, "I'd rather you show me first."

Well, I had it to do, so I set my light and gun down beside a tree. I came up quick in a couple or three strides as I was hollering, "Mitzie! Mitzie!" I pushed him just enough that he grabbed me. I went to twisting and kicking, all the time hollering, "Catch him! Catch him!" It was a moonlit night, and he was keeping me between him and Ol' Mitzie. She had made a couple of moves and was growling, showing her teeth. When I finally broke loose from him, I went to the ground on my knees, lunging forward at him, slapping the ground with both hands. She must have been going for his throat, for she jumped high at his head. He pushed her away but was quickly hollering, "Mitzie! Mitzie!" She crouched, showing teeth and growling as he put his hand out. He was snapping his fingers as he kept saying, "Mitzie!" She jumped, barely missing his hand. When this sorry, no-good sucker went to hollering, "Call her off! Call her off!" I said, "You ain't bit yet."

He said, "I believe you. Call her off."

"You're the kind who's got to be showed and can't be told nothing. Quit crying like a baby and take your medicine like a man."

"Call her off."

Now, I knew he had a knife, but I had a gun. So before things got out of whack, I spoke to Ol' Mitzie, for this ain't the way to hang it up.

SNORE MARKS

A lot of water has run under the bridge since the days that I sold Moorman feed. T.R. Moorman was a chemist who scientifically formulated minerals, vitamins, and nine different proteins into a block for cattle. The cattle consumption was controlled by the hardness of the block. This was a high-dollar synthetic feed that could outperform all other feeds.

Now, it had been twenty-five years or more since I'd sold this supplemental feed. I hadn't thought about minerals and vitamins being supplemental in people's lives until I heard this old veterinarian doctor, who called himself a food nutritionist, talking on the radio. It was more by accident than on purpose that I was caught listening to this talk show. The title of this show was *Dead Doctors Don't Lie*. Not being a fan of doctors or lawyers, I thought I would see what this one had to say and if he was any different from the others. After listening to this fellow talk, I decided he was in the same business that I'd been in selling feed, except that he was selling supplemental minerals and vitamins for the health care of people. I'd done the same thing selling feed for cattle.

It took me a couple of months or maybe a half dozen more times of listening to this fellow talk before trying this product of minerals and vitamins extracted from plants that are supposed to be more compatible than other vitamins. I wondered how I'd be able to tell if this product was really helping me. I didn't think what I had was a health problem. Neither did I want to admit that it's called "being plain sorry." I ain't never liked to work; cowboying around or hunting fits my style. It doesn't bother me not having all the conveniences of this world, not in the least bit.

After taking this product for a month, all I'll say about it is that I'm glad this stuff wasn't around when I was a kid. Had my dad known about it, he would have worked me to death! I needed to restock my monthly supply when I called this old mineral man who sold this stuff. He was married to a nice, pretty, younger lady; however, he was quite humorous himself. So I'm going to pause here and put a warning label on this tale. Now this could be a tale; I'm not really sure—you decide.

Like I said, this old mineral man had a very nice, pretty, younger wife. When I went over to restock my monthly supply, I don't remember the exact words in the conversation, but this old mineral man might have had a little gimp in his get-along.

I didn't understand or make any connection with what he said about "Snore marks! I didn't even know I snored."

I cocked my head, knowing I heard what he said. It just didn't make sense. He then went on to say something about waking up one morning the week before. He said that his legs were sore and ached like he'd been walking for miles. Not wanting to complain but getting around slowly, he came back into the bedroom after putting on the coffee.

He sat down on the bed and was rubbing his legs when he said to his wife, "I must have walked for hours in my sleep last night, for when I woke up this morning both of my legs were awful sore."

He said he never understood what she meant when she said, "Snore marks!" I didn't understand either, but I didn't say nothing. So he went on with the conversation and said, "This morning when I woke up, my leg was hurting, and I wondered if I was dreaming last night about being kicked by a mule. When I went to get up out of bed and go fix coffee, I nearly fell down. Then as I steadied my legs under me, I finally got a chance to examine my leg, and there I found a big, round, red mark." He said, "I turned and looked at my wife. She smiled and said, 'Snore marks!'"

WHEELER DEALER

$\mathscr{I}$ started operating a wild hog-buying station at the first of 2008. The company buys hogs sixty pounds and up, but they don't buy nothing smaller than sixty pounds. Now, on either side of where the loading or unloading chute connects to the weighing scale, there is a small crack three inches wide, for nothing is permitted to touch the scale. A big hog cannot escape, but a small pig can squeeze through.

It was barely good daylight when Mr. J.H. (Dumpy) Dickson and his wife drove up to my place. I'd finished feeding my old dogs and horses and went directly up to the hog pen. Dumpy had a hard time getting squared up to the unloading chute. I noticed that he had eight or ten smaller pigs in with those hogs, so I mentioned the crack and that they'd probably get out. He was protecting a hole with a board stuck in it and working the slide gate on his trailer all at the same time. He told me that he thought he could hold the pig on the trailer. So without a hot shot, I went to trying to make those bigger hogs unload. But they piled up in the front end of his closed-in trailer, and I was having problems getting hogs to unpile. He'd worked the sliding trailer gate a couple of times and had stopped a small pig from getting out when finally one of the bigger hogs took that hole like a bullet, with a pig following it. Dumpy wasn't able to stop the pig, and he never slowed down but hit the crack by the scale and was out and gone.

Dumpy said, "Oh! Did you see that? That pig went straight out that crack, and I was supposed to let a friend have those pigs."

I said, "If you want 'em, I'll go to the house and get my dogs."

He said, "I don't have time. Furthermore, it's no telling where that pig would go."

It just so happened that my neighbor's wife, Brittney Wells, was out getting her morning exercise when her little dog bayed that pig in the Singleton cemetery. Brittney and Bo have both hunted with me. They've seen me catch hogs, and she knew there wasn't nothing to it. Now she was presented with the opportunity to have been the hero of the day. But she thought better of it and let the pig get away.

I said to Dumpy, "I've got a pig in the pen about that pig's size."

"How much do you want for your pig?"

I said, "Fifteen dollars. Are you buying or just selling?"

As he reached into his pocket for his billfold, he said, "I guess I'm wheeling and dealing, for I need that pig for my friend for a barbecue."

I'll say this for ol' J.H. "Dumpy" Dixon: he didn't come here to rob or steal; he came here to wheel and deal. Now, what a lot of folks don't know is that the pig will come back to those hogs that it knows are in my pen. After a day or two I'd taken my old dogs, caught that pig, and put it back into my pen.

I sell, swap, or trade these fat pigs for dog food that I buy at Sam's. That used to be about the price of a good fat pig. You gotta have a little come-on to be able to roll up, especially if you want to wheel and deal.

EMPTY-HANDED

The plan of life seems simple for a cowboy; he comes into this world looking for a good horse and the right kind of dog. When he's old enough to get his driver's license and drive around, he's looking for a rig. After he's old enough to get his rig, he begins thinking of his own setup. Getting that first piece of real estate and getting the improvements is a monumental test.

The hands that I've known down through the years of my life were all content with being a cowboy. But most don't understand that they were called to this position of life: that their real purpose in life is to honor and glorify God. What's stranger even yet is that a lot of church people don't know that either.

Consider yourself fortunate if someone has loved you enough to have taken time to share with you the love of Jesus Christ by sharing with you their own personal testimony; that's called their witness. Now, that's God's way for us to serve him. When we are used as a witness for the LORD Jesus Christ, his Spirit and his Word draws a lost person to realize they're lost in their sin. Our sin separates us from God. To die lost in sin means eternal separation from God, condemned because they have not believed in the name of the

only begotten Son of God. To live is only to look unto the LORD
Jesus Christ, to accept by faith the payment that Jesus made in full
on the cross for your sin personally, then to trust in Jesus completely
and place your faith upon Him, calling upon the name of Jesus for
salvation. This is how a personal relationship begins; a transformation that takes place and is known as the new birth.

To do business with God is by far the most important business
of our life, and right close behind this is telling others how we've
come to this saving knowledge. It honors God when we obey Him.
It glorifies God when someone trusts Jesus as Savior and LORD. It's
a privilege and honor to work in God's field, but it will test your
metal. The choice that we make about serving God may well deter-
mine life or death, heaven or hell, in someone else's life that God
holds us accountable for. Don't walk away empty-handed; let someone who loves you help disciple you to become everything God has
called and has purposed you to be. When we serve God His way, it
will bring him praise, honor, and glory. To love Jesus's way demands
our total obedience, our all.

THREE DIFFERENT SETUPS

*N*ow, my first milestone in this cowboy life came in 1962 at the age of seventeen years old. I had paid cash for my first rig, a new Chevrolet truck and an Ed Handover gooseneck trailer. I had some rough old lease pastures, and the stocker cow prices had remained relatively low. I was never able to exchange the cattle for any sizable amount of property to start my first setup.

I was twenty-six years old and married a pretty sixteen-year-old gal. We moved into a duplex apartment, but I was not satisfied living in town. I was presented an opportunity a year later to move to an old ranch home and was given the usage of a large trap to keep my horses in. No one was living on the ranch prior to this, and the landowners wanted someone to keep an eye on things. It's been said that two can live as cheap as one. I don't know how they figured this mathematical problem, for I was struggling to pay all the bills. Although when two agree and want the same things in life, it just may be possible. For Jonah got along in the belly of the whale, Daniel in the lion's den, but I know a man that didn't get along and won't get a chance again. I leased two hundred acres from Mr. Gue Ray, who offered to sell me the property for three hundred dollars per acre, no money down, 6%

interest. I was paying three dollars per acre lease per year. Interest on the money kept me from owning the land and making a good deal. The place sold that same year for five hundred dollars per acre.

My mother and dad were always aware and concerned about what was going on in my life. They offered to give me one hundred acres of my inheritance. It was not appreciated by the rest of my family, but Mom and Dad done as they pleased.

This transpired in the third year of our marriage. Cattle prices had gone up, and I began culling hard on my herd. I was burning the candle at both ends, building barns, corrals, and fences, day working, bull trading, and trading horses and training dogs, along with whatever else it took to tree the coon. That fall I had enough money saved to start a contractor to build a new three-bedroom brick home on the land that I had inherited. After having a water well drilled, building a forty by seventy-foot pole barn, stock pens, and net wire traps, I had an extremely nice setup and should have been content.

A form of coal, called lignite, was discovered from Singleton to Piedmont, and I had it under my property. This made the value of the land soar to over two thousand dollars per acre, an unheard of amount in 1980.

In 1981 I made a land exchange for my setup in Texas for the Old Box P Ranch, a very good half-section of land in southeastern Oklahoma that had a one-year-old four-bedroom home on it. I finally got my setup established into a yearling operation, with two lease pastures that were used for the cow and calf operation, and one other place where I only had my horses and mules. Business came to a halt at the end of 1992. A divorce shut down my operations, and I found out it's a lot harder coming down the ladder than it was going up.

I was back in Texas in 1993 and would have liked to turn hermit; however, I found that you never get through paying for your mistakes, and after three years I came out of my shell and went back to catching hogs. It took the whole year of 1997 to build a log house that doesn't get much attention but is low efficient.

Lloyd Perry
Singleton Jr.

TRADE DAY

First Monday trade day was, for many years, a common, useful gathering for country folks; but the old traditions slowly began to give way to the changing of these modern times. Now, while I was living in eastern Oklahoma in the early 1990s, I'd heard tell of a place over in Arkansas called County Line that held a trade day every Monday. So I eased over into that country to have a look-see, and I found it to be an auction sale barn that sold no stocker cattle, only a few milk cows, milk goats, a few sheep, and hogs. A good many work horses and mules then a regular horse sale followed. Outside under several big trees was an assortment of rigs packed with all kinds of trade goods. Some folks wanted cash, but most of the folks enjoyed having a good trade.

In the summer of 1991, I went to work at the McAlester Sale Barn, one of the bigger and better sale barns that I ever worked or sold stock at. My time started at seven o'clock on Sunday morning; but being the part of a Christian, I asked my boss, Mr. George Tarr, before taking the job, "I've been doing business with God for a lot of years between eleven and twelve o'clock on Sundays. Would it be possible that I could take my dinner hour then and go to church?"

Mr. George Tarr just looked up, sort of surprised, and said he didn't have a problem with that. I worked at the sale barn only a short time and saw a lot of folks at the sale barn that I'd also seen in church. They went out of their way to make me feel welcome at church and at the sale barn.

Mr. George gave me a job that took a little cow savvy. I helped three other men sort and bring up cattle, and because I came from over the mountain fifty miles away and stayed at the sale barn on Sunday nights, I was offered the job of staying on the clock straight through from Sunday morning until the sale was over Monday night or Tuesday morning, whichever the case. After working straight through and then driving home, several of the boys had begun telling me to be careful and not go to sleep and not have a wreck, to just pull over and take a nap.

I'd made it nearly a year, barely making it in. Each week I dragged my trailer with me. I'd usually buy a ton of feed and put it in the front end of the trailer, and Mr. George would let me go inside and bid on something I wanted to buy. I'd usually get a trade horse or a few rannies (small calves).

I'd been there several months when I was called in to work the ring. I didn't know what happened to the other ring hand; I thought I was just filling in. But the third week I told my boss, Mr. Tarr, that I knew a ring man made more money, and rightly so because he stayed busy the whole time. If they stuck me in there, I needed to be subsidized. He said he'd look into it and get back with me. I was told I was in a place so that I could buy stock, and being as I was on straight time, there wouldn't be no extra money. That went against the grain.

After working one of those big, long sales and having gone to sleep on my way home, I lost my trailer and a load of feed in a wreck, but I managed to get the truck back up on the road. The next week I went into the ring with an attitude and didn't stay long. It's the cowboy way—to be here today and gone tomorrow. It didn't bother me losing my job for what I thought was right. Up until now nobody ever knew the rest of that story.

A couple of weeks before this wreck, I was working in the ring, and for a cattle sale they sold a lot of horses at this sale barn. I didn't know a lot of those horse traders by name, but I recognized 'em and would have known their hides in a hide house. Now, there was a young wheeler-dealer that I'd seen around but had never had any dealings with. I took him for a shyster and wouldn't buy any of his stories. It had spooked my mule when he introduced this little eight hundred-pound horse. The horse was smooth and small but looked like a regular horse that had been turned out, for he wasn't cleaned up.

The story was, "He's young and would make a dandy kid horse."

One thing I learned at a right early age was that if you were going to do business, you have got to have some stock. I was never able to own but a couple of trade horses at a time. I was always under-financed and on this shoestring operation that had more bills than it had income. Now, I let the ring man who was being paid do the honors of jumping up on that horse. But the horse didn't show anything wrong other than, like me, he didn't know much. I read way too much into this ol' pony, for I saw 'em dressed up and ringing a bell (making a lot of money).

I've been accused of being narrow-minded about having things my way and being partial to the King James Bible. I don't apologize for the King James Bible, for it's the one I was saved under. I've also been faulted for not over complimenting anyone. So I give a little credit to my son, Scott. When he was young he acted like he wanted to help me, but I didn't want to get him hurt and did my own horseback riding myself. Now, when I came in with this ol' pony that I'll called Ol' Kid, Scott wanted to ride him, so we put him in a powder river panel lot (stock panels). Scott was riding Ol' Kid while I caught up another horse; we then rode off into the pasture. Scott got down to open and shut a gap, but when he was getting back on, Ol' Kid downed his head and showed his stuff. Scott made a half-dozen hard, high jumps without his right stirrup. Scott probably carried him farther than I could have under those conditions. I couldn't do anything but head that ol' pony. When he hit the ground, I rode up and asked, "Are you hurt?" I suppose I could have said, "That was a mighty good ride," or "I thought you had 'er made," or "You looked pretty sticky." The truth is after knowing that Scott wasn't hurt, I was really down on myself for not smelling a rat and not knowing this ol' pony was only pen broke. I couldn't see this hole in 'em that was a mile wide. I knew this dude was a shyster and that a tree doesn't fall far from its stump.

I caught this ol' pony and snubbed 'em up, and we went back to the house with one thing on my mind: I intended to put this bronc back in that pen, set up on his back, and whip the buck out of 'em. Strange—when it was over, I couldn't make this horse buck in that pen; I was kind of glad that things went that way, for whipping and riding can get a might western. It was bad enough that I was sure to lose a hundred dollars if I resold him; however, to get broke up or crippled up would have added insult to injury. So I stuck Ol' Kid in the back forty with hay and water and figured I was bound to figure out something next spring.

It was nearly June. Ol' Kid had gotten fat and had shed off his winter coat and was now a pretty dark bay. White markings were the same, but he was a nine hundred-pound hoss. I talked my plan over with Mr. Bea Mendenhall, who was ninety-two years old, then offered to sell him half interest in this horse cheap if he would help me.

Bea said, "No, I won't buy in, but I'll be the shyster." Bea pulled a dollar out of his pocket and bought into the action so that neither of us would be lying.

I brought Ol' Kid back to the house to start the procedure of dressing up a bronc. Now, I don't guess he'd ever had so many little things done to him, for he resisted and fought most of the things that I put on him. He stayed in a dry lot on grain; and whether it was morning, noon, or night, I devoted a little time, if not a whole lot of time, until I slowly began to see him come around. In just a little over two weeks, I kind of had him where he would ride around. It's not my way to spur and jerk, but there's a time when I think it's necessary. If I do, I want to be out of that horse's mouth with a bow saw or something around the horse's nose. I had just the thing—a little chain that was fastened to a curb strap under his chin. Mr. Jim Ellis had given me this nosepiece. I cowboyed up and was able to rake 'em on either side at just the right time. When Ol' Kid started coming around, I hurried up a cowboy handle on 'em with a loose rein in a small pen.

Now, the dude that sold me this bronc went to the County Line horse sale. I was hoping to re-introduce him to Ol' Kid. If he didn't recognize Ol' Kid at the first sight, I was sure he'd remember 'em later. This dude was still young and going to trading school. Sometimes getting an education can be expensive. The test of losing money in a profession you love can test your character.

It was a long way from where I lived to the County Line horse sale, and at ninety-two years old, Mr. Bea Mendenhall in his own fascinating way introduced Ol' Kid. When Ol' Kid came into the ring, Bea got up to make sure that the number on the horse was the same as the number we'd checked in.

One of the two owners of the sale barn, a fellow named Mr. Jimmy, who was starting this stock, came over to Bea, looked at the billing, and said, "That's him. What's the story?"

Bea said, "Yes, sir, he's a nice-looking little horse, but he's too much hoss for me." Bea reached into his pocket and pulled out his money clip and said to the ring hand, "Here." He offered the ring hand twenty dollars to ride this horse around.

The ring hand said, "No, sir. I can't take your money. They pay me to ride 'em."

Bea said, "Well, then, let's see you make him operate."

With that, the ring hand swung up on Ol' Kid. As he jumped him forward, he hooked (spurred) Ol' Kid! You couldn't make him buck in a pen. With a light neck rein, Ol' Kid was coming back under himself, left and right several times as fast as a horse can operate in a ring. He then spun 'em around tight. Then Mr. Jimmy told the ring hand to pull up and see if he'd handle slow and easy. Ol' Kid had a lot of practice in a pen and could operate any way you liked.

Now, I was standing in the back of the barn, watching this dude as he came up close to have a good look at Ol' Kid. A shyster is not a horseman and doesn't know horses. But if he did recognize Ol' Kid, he'd never seen him operate like this.

So the dude said to the auctioneer, "Ask 'em if a kid could ride this horse."

Now, Bea and I had anticipated this, and at ninety-two years old, Bea put on a performance himself and did a super job. As he just stood there, Mr. Jimmy came over and asked Mr. Bea the same question.

Bea said to 'em, "Well, now, that I wouldn't know. Tell 'em that I ain't got no kids."

Laughing, Mr. Jimmy repeated what Bea said, and that raised the roof.

The auctioneer said to the dude, "Does that answer your question?"

The dude shook his head and said, "No."

Mr. Jimmy had set this ol' pony in for a lot more money than I'd paid for 'em, and there was a couple folks bidding on 'em. This ring man was close to this dude when the dude said he wanted to see 'em operate again. I knew this ring man's intentions when he hung his hooks into Ol' Kid to see if he'd kick out (buck), but Ol' Kid wouldn't buck in a close pen. He just jumped way out there, and knew to come back with or without any help from the ring man. Ol' Kid had been jerked around, and he didn't need any help to come back. The ring man didn't anticipate Ol' Kid's hard comeback and had bowed over a little bit behind and out of position. Being a little bit behind, he had to pull Ol' Kid up.

Then Mr. Jimmy smiled and said, "I see what that old man meant."

This ring man was a horseman, and he woke Ol' Kid up and made 'em ride around.

This dude couldn't stand it any longer, and at the last minute before the auctioneer sold out, he got into the bidding. Now, I had all the intentions in the world of running Ol' Kid up on this dude, but the thought had left just like it had come, for Ol' Kid was a lot higher now than when he was set in. The thought of messing up a mission accomplished caused me to lose my nerve, and instead of bidding, I was grinning, for Ol' Kid was returning to his original owner. It wasn't long after my grinning that the word *false* hit me where I live. Now, a false representation doesn't wear any better on me than buying a false appearance. What I did was wrong and is called coming short of God's glory by settling a score myself instead of obeying God's Word, Romans 12:19 (KJV): "Dearly beloved, avenge not yourselves, but rather give place unto wrath: for it is written, Vengeance is mine; I will repay, saith the LORD." So I told myself, *If you believe the Bible, then why aren't you living it?*

Are you aware of the truth of God's Word and how its application applies to everyday life? Sin always carries a consequence. A failed test of God is usually one test that you get to do over. The test of God, or to prove you, is not to see if you will fail.

ICING ON THE CAKE

It's not often this old-time cowboy ever gets off his home range and takes in any new territory. But it just so happened that I went to side (to be there for) a friend at a funeral in another church. I call myself dressed up in a clean, starched shirt and blue jeans, but if I'm seen wearing a dress jacket in the hot summertime, I'm headed for a funeral, or else I'm on my way to get married. I was dressed up when I unloaded out of my old Dodge diesel truck that's been a cowboy's Cadillac. When I looked at my watch I noticed I was running a little early. So I decided to go inside and find a cool place to shade up.

I happened to see this lady drive up in a pickup. That struck me as being unusual, seeing this well-dressed lady get out of this truck. I thought, *She's a rancher's wife, or else she's a widow.* Being a stranger to that part of the country, it was natural that when I got to the door, like any good cowboy, I grabbed my hat, opened the door, and stepped back, giving her the onceover, looking for any brand of ownership.

When I didn't see any ring, I smiled and said, "How are you today, ma'am?"

There wasn't any doubt that that smile was of a Texan when she said, "Fine, and how are you?"

Being as I don't have any pearly whites up front, I only lip-smiled and answered her saying, "Ma'am, I'm doing just fine." She smiled again as she went on inside the building.

There were maybe a dozen folks scattered around visiting. I found a cool place and sat down, thinking that I could spoil pretty easy to this refrigerated air. Then from somewhere this beaut' appeared and took a seat, visiting with a couple of older ladies a couple rows ahead of me. Now, my eyes were taken in by the beauty of her sun-darkened skin and long, black hair. All of a sudden, she turned her head, looked at me, and smiled. That made me nervous and very uncomfortable, and I wanted to go somewhere, but instead I looked down at my boots and thought, *Oh, boy, you crazy, ugly glute, do you really think a decent lady like that would even notice the likes of you? You've got about as much chance with someone like that as a long-legged pullet in a coyote den.*

Now, I live by the code of the West, and it puts a decent woman on a high pedestal. Good women are scarce as gold and much more highly valued. A decent woman is to be treasured and to be protected from all that is thought dirty or raw and/or unpleasant. In my time, a cowboy tipped his hat at a decent lady and held himself afar.

I am thankful for the life God's allowed me to live as a cowboy. Yet if it gets unbearably lonely, I won't be walking away. I'll search for a decent woman to side me; that'll be the icing on the cake.

DOUBLE DIPPER

$\mathscr{I}$t seems like it's been years ago since I'd sent pictures of me and a few big hogs to my grandchildren. Then after Christmas I started writing down some of these old bygone yarns. When my son-in-law Jack started having Jackie Ann take pictures of their big hogs and they sent 'em to me, I enjoyed seeing and hearing about their achievements with their dogs and horses. So when I didn't have a good hog's picture to send them back, I'd send 'em a yarn, but as soon as I could, I'd send 'em both for a little double dip.

Now, I'd mailed 'em a double dipper when I got a phone call from Jackie Ann, who said, "Your grandson Ethan has all the pictures of his Paw Paw Perry's hogs spread out in the floor, and he's astonished with his Paw's big hogs. Your son-in-law is sitting at the table rereading the story that you just sent, and he's astonished also."

So I said, "You called to check 'em out and see if they're authentic, is that right?"

Now she laughed. I knew that she wouldn't tell me, for I'd figured her out and had hit the nail on the head.

So I said, "You know Texas is big country, and those old hogs go with the territory. But that ain't what you called about; it's the story that you're wondering about. Yes! It's true, for you know Lee don't allow no fabrication of the truth.

"Now, here's the way that I put it all together: I didn't see any mark of ownership, but with that long, coal black hair and a smile like that, she had to be somebody's wife. Else men would have been buzzing around her like bees. Now, she knew she was pretty and a little flirty, for she didn't mind embarrassing me. I didn't ask her or anybody what her name was, nor have I seen her since, but if I ever see that smile again, well, I'll try and get the rest of the story for you."

Being a Christian cowboy, I've tried to use my old horses, dogs, and even these old life railway experiences as a tool that God's placed into my hand to help point others (especially those who know me) toward a personal relationship with the LORD Jesus Christ. It's called being reconciled to God.

This relationship starts with salvation. Through being discipled, the relationship continues as Jesus is made LORD of life. When we yield and submit unto the control of the Holy Spirit, it's quite a life when you're able to have the best of both, now and forever.

Lloyd Perry
Singleton, Tex

BUTTER FACE

Every now and again I get a bad case of the down-yonders. I get homesick and mighty lonesome for a lot of the old-timers and a way of life lived long ago when one old-timer would tell their own tale and then another one would do his best to try and top it. These old-timers were the objects of these tales. Everybody assumed it to be true and funny, for folks would all laugh with you and not at you.

I'm glad that I got to live out some of the last days of the Old West. It's been said by some older than me that they too were around in those good old days and they didn't miss 'em. Be that as it may, all changes aren't for the good. I remember when vulgar talk would have got it put on you so bad that the man riding the white horse from Ajax couldn't have taken it off. Four-letter words weren't spoken in public, and they were not funny. I regret to say that we now live in a different day and age; therefore, I will stay true to what I tried to instill into my children. It is dangerous to embellish truth. I have often said, "If it ain't true, it ain't worth telling"; therefore, this may not be worth telling, and on the other hand, it may be true.

Now, I heard an old boy talking about some gal he called "Butter Face." Someone asked, "How did she ever get the name 'Butter

Face'?" He replied, "She looked pretty good everywhere but her face!"

For better or worse, I remembered that story and probably should have left it alone, knowing it wasn't worth telling. I forgot about my own advice and took in too much territory. I told this tale to a cute little thing who's a friend of mine. When I finished telling this tale, she wouldn't say nothing. I thought a bolt of lightning may have hit her. Knowing I'd already said too much, I didn't dare laugh either. Realizing I'd made a mistake in sharing this tale, I wanted to but couldn't afford to say, "Honey, you know that ain't you." I was in a nine-line bind. With my fat in the fire, I finally broke that deafening silence by saying, "Hello! Hell-lo!"

She finally said, "I didn't realize you were through."

Real low, I said, "That's it; you know it's just a tale."

Very professional-like, she gave a pretty good belly laugh then said, "You know, I've always enjoyed our little conversations."

Now, I don't remember what she said next, but I do remember her saying, "Good-bye!"

AJAX

*H*aving spent a good many hours in a saddle, I had a lot of time to think about how I could make this carefree lifestyle of mine pan out. Most hobbies are for money folk, and I cut all the ones I thought I couldn't afford. That narrowed it down to just one hobby, dominoes, and I thought I knew 'em backwards and forwards. When you play 'em and not just lay 'em, they do their own talking. This I've learned, it's always better to humble yourself then have the LORD do it for you. Now, I like to have a good time and might in fun say, "I might not know my ABCs, but I do know my 123s," or some other old talk.

I only had three head of horses in my string—Ol' Blue, my favorite mount; a big-footed, jug-headed, blue mare that was good in the woods; and a brown performance horse I'd gotten from a cutting horse trainer, Mr. Knight, in Conroe, Texas. This horse was good at sorting cattle in a pen but wasn't much in the pasture. He wasn't doing enough to pay his way either, and I'd decided he might be better at being a play day horse than as a using horse.

I knew only one horse-trading woman who switched several good using horses and cutting horses over to play day horses and sold 'em high, Mrs. Narcissi Moriarty. Like any good horse trader, she bought 'em cheap and sold 'em high. That didn't bother me that bad, until she wanted to put an old white horse off on me. As soon as I saw him, I said, "Where'd you get old Ajax?"

She kind of grinned when she realized what I was talking about, and she said, "He's a good using horse that's got one bad fault: he kicks."

I told her in a case like that, she could weigh him as easy as me. Now, I don't guess she quite figured it like I did. I had an opportunity to trade for that keen longhorn head and shoulder mount that she had hung over her fireplace that day. I liked that head mount, but I really didn't have no place to put it. After that opportunity, I never had a chance to trade for it again. So, with too little to boot and a horse that I really didn't want, I rode off from her place and left the old brown horse there.

Ol' Ajax proved to be a good using horse, and not long after I owned him, I roped an extremely wild, bad cow off of him. While two or three others had taken a good raking from this sharp-horned cow, I could turn Ol' Ajax's back end, and he could dot an *i* or cross a *t*. After a while, I got tired of watching out for my old dogs. If one came in behind me, I'd pull Ol' Ajax over out of a trail and let the dog pass by, for if I didn't, he would have probably killed all of my dogs, or else he was going to make 'em stop following me. But the straw that broke the camel's back was when he kicked the trailer gate as I walked up to get him out. The next Saturday, we eased down to the Navasota Livestock Auction. I had this kid that worked in the ring to jump up on him bareback and ride 'em around.

When the auctioneer asked if anybody had a story, I never said a word and was hoping Ol' Ajax would keep his secret also. However, Mr. Sonny Moore must have smelled a rat or something, for he asked, "Does he kick?" as he popped the whip on the back of Ol' Ajax's tail end. Ol' Ajax jumped and kicked out with both hind feet.

I heard somebody say, "Whoo, does he!"

I hollered back and said, "Only about the price!"

Lloyd Perry
Singleton, Tx.

FOOLED BY A FEELING

*N*ow, I like a horse that's gentle, dependable, and trustworthy, but my dogs are a little different deal. There's only one kind of dog that has ever suited me, those called one-man dogs. But every now and then my breeding program gets turned around, and my old dogs get gentle and my horse gets spooky (or kind of crazy).

When I was a young man I had improvised a plan. I intended to own an iser (a horse that can do it all) and have two trade horses for my backup horses. Now, I realize that if you can cowboy, you can cowboy on a mule; however, if you're cowboying on an iser, you can make the rest of those jugheads holler uncle. It seems like back then there were a lot more good dogs than there were good horses. Today it's turned around: nearly everyone is riding an extremely good horse, and there are very few extremely good dogs.

In my time I've had six isers and six extremely good dogs. I hardly will trade on an iser or an extremely good dog but keep 'em till they either get old or else I sell them high. Now, I'd taken a four-year-old gray mare in on a trade that made a woods horse deluxe that I hog-hunted on. Later I bought a five-year-old cutting mare. Both of my backup trade horses were mares and were better-than-average horses. I got it in my head or had this feeling that I could raise better horses than I was trading for. So I bred my mares to a black stud horse that my brother Hershel gave my brother Jim. The gray mare had a red roan horse colt, and the sorrel mare had a bay horse colt. These colts were still studs coming two years old in the spring. I was working steady that fall building pole barns when Mr. Bill Bay asked me about my colts. We made a trade that he would get 'em broke, cut 'em, ride 'em, and feed 'em until spring. I was to pick one and give him the other. It turned out kind of a bad deal. The one I felt like should have been the nicest horse wouldn't break out but was crazier than a road lizard.

The bronc stomper handling these horses said, "That roan bronc likes to buck. Don't spit off that roan." He said he'd rather ease his hand up to his mouth, spit in his hand, and rub it on his pants than to fight that bronc.

A FAVORITE

$\mathscr{I}$ was on the business end of a hoe, working in my garden. It was hot enough to have melted my tallow, so I pulled up for a breath of fresh air. As I wiped away the sweat, I began to recall when I was a young cowboy how I hated garden work. I'd called it common work, and Dad set me straight.

When he cleared his throat to make sure we made eye contact, he began saying, "There's a lot more to owning and running a ranch than what's done from the back of a horse. You need to learn what I can show you and other things also."

I answered him by saying, "Yes, sir. I know and understand what you're saying. There's just got to be an easier way than this."

Dad just stood there holding the end of that hoe, looking a long time before shaking his head. Then he said, "If there is, I ain't found it. You've got to eat."

Now, I know for a fact that it's hard to understand a cowboy, young or old. Unless you've been cut from that mold, he's different. Cowboys are born, not made. That brought to mind a conversation I'd heard just recently. I'd seen little Scott McDougal, who was two or three years old at the time, who didn't want to wear his church clothes. He thought he ought to have been able to wear his boots and hat to the occasion.

A smile appeared as I recalled a similar occasion that happened to me when my mom came at me with a pair of sawed-off britches and said, "Put these on, for you'll be much cooler in these."

I don't recall my age, but I know I was out of diapers and into long pants. With both eyes bugged out and steadily backing up, I answered her saying, "No, ma'am! I don't want to wear that." Even at a young age, this was below my dignity.

In her disgust, she said, "Just put 'em on."

All of the excitement must have spooked my mule and caused a run-away. Now, after a good shalleying (whipping), the next time she came at me I stayed hitched. I never looked up or said one word; I just stood there with my head down, for I'd made up my mind that even if I had to take another whipping, I wasn't wearing those shorts, and I wasn't going to cry. I determined this a long time before I knew exactly how to put it into words. I haven't compromised the principle—that's below the dignity of any good cowboy to dress up like a dude.

I'M PROUD OF YOU

I was killing time in a laid-back way while in a conversation with another old-timer who's a friend of mine. While in our conversation, he began telling me about how proud he was of his wife. Immediately, I thought of something smart-aleck to say but instead said, "Is that right?"

He reiterated that conversation by saying, "Oh, y'all!" She had won three awards and a large amount of cash at their last year's Christmas banquet; however, the place where she works didn't make any mention of the woman's husband. He didn't think it was right.

I said, "Really?" But I could tell he was dead serious about this.

He went on telling me that he knew they paid his wife well, even when she had to do overtime or work a double shift. But he also worked a long ten-hour day running a bulldozer. It'd be late when he got in. He'd be awful tired. When he'd get home, there would be no supper and no wife.

I said, "I know the feeling."

The company my friend works for also had a Christmas party last year. His boss man made a short speech, recognizing both the men and their wives. After congratulating the men on their best year ever, the company gave each man's wife fifty-dollar Christmas checks to boot. I said, "Amazing! Imagine that!"

This needs a warning label, for I told him a tale about an ol' timer. This ol' timer had gotten long in the tooth with more years behind him than he now cared to remember. He had her made, just living on easy street. Both he and his wife's eyes were getting dim now, and their hearing was getting dull. He just rocked in his chair and did some thinking about their life together. He'd never shown his wife much consideration. The more he thought about it, he hadn't shown her much affection either. But the more he rocked and thought, the harder it was to put thoughts into words.

Finally the ol' coot couldn't take it any longer. He just blurted out, "I'm proud of you!"

His wife answered, "Y'all! And I'm tired of you too!"

CONGRATULATIONS, HOG

The home of a wild hog is usually a dark, thick place. Now, there's a lot of different kinds of thickets. Any time you're down belly crawling and have to get within ten to twenty feet of your work, it's bad. But most thickets aren't that big, as compared to the three thousand acres of yaupon thicket on the south side of my old home range.

Now, I'd had a flash that I didn't like skinning any more hogs than I had sold. The hog market had gone up: a two hundred-pound hog would bring fifty cents a pound live. I was getting forty-five and skinning 'em then icing them down and hauling them to someone's house who might want credit. The catching way was more appealing to me. Only I didn't have a bulldog.

I knew a fellow who had hog dogs and a couple of catch dogs. I went over and visited this fellow, and he had a young bulldog that he'd only used a couple of times on hogs. When I asked how much, he told me to take her and use her as long as I liked and when I got through with her, just bring her back. Now, I've been up the creek and over the hill a few times. I know that everything shiny ain't gold.

In a few days I had an opportunity to try this young bulldog gyp on a sow that weighed around 175 pounds. She nailed this hog, but not by the ear like she was supposed to do. That puzzled me some, but it didn't spook my mule too bad. I got the sow tied but was going to have to wait until the dog bite healed before I could sell her.

Now, it's a handful to catch a hog by yourself. I talked this over with my brother Hershel. He agreed to let me turn the catch dog loose and catch a hog, but when they broke bay, he'd start shooting, for Hershel could shoot a hog as good running as I could with them standing.

We were over toward Bedias in the old Sproggins bottom, where Cain Creek runs into South Bedias Creek. Now, there are forty to sixty acres in and along these creeks, and in the richest soil there grows wild lemons. They are real thick, tall, and thorny. The only passage is a game trail, and on a lot of it you're on your belly crawling. If you hear a buzzing, rattling sound, you hope it's in front of you. You can't turn around or get up, so you push backwards as fast as you can and get out of there.

We'd come around an old field on the northwest side of South Bedias Creek when we struck sign of one lone big hog. He had been rooting out in a field. I was packing iron (gun) in a sling, leading this bulldog gyp. Our dogs had gone on west as we followed. In fifteen minutes, our dogs bayed, and it was in a good place that was kind of open. We'd seen this old hog as he'd run at a dog. He looked to be probably a 225 to 250-pound hog. I had a big smile, for one hundred twenty-five dollars was fixing to be money in my pocket, so I thought.

I set my gun beside a tree, turned that bulldog gyp loose, and wasn't but a few steps behind her when she caught that hog behind the ear. He jumped and spun around, giving that bulldog a sling. This big hog was all bowed up, looking straight at me, when Ol' Bunt hit him in the rear end. He turned and ran off the other way. It all happened quickly. I was less than twenty feet away from this hog. This bulldog was now yipping behind these dogs as this hog pulled freight.

This all happened a little after eight o'clock in the morning. This old hog liked to have walked me and Hershel to death after that. He'd run awhile, stop, then trot. He'd taken us nearly to Singleton as he went out of hearing distance toward Shiro. It was after dinner when he came back toward us, but we failed to see him. As this hog went back to the lemon thicket, he stayed bayed for a while and then pulled out toward Bedias. I left Hershel and went back to where we first bayed him. I'd just crossed a branch when I heard the dogs coming toward me. I got behind a tree and waited on this hog and gunned him down when he came by. It was two o'clock in the afternoon.

When I saw Hershel, he stuck out his hand and said to me, "Congratulations."

I smiled, shaking my head, wondering what he meant. The way I'd seen it, there went one hundred twenty-five dollars down the drain!

WRECKS

In the past few months we've had a run of wrecks. The last one was when my four-wheeler came unstrapped, rolling back and causing one of my dogs, called Ol' Jess, to jump out and be drug; however, she'd come through that ordeal okay.

Another wreck happened when Skeeter and I bayed up a hog next to a slue, with a lot of open ground around it. He went around to cut the hog off as I went to the dogs. As I got there, the hog tried to run, and the dogs caught it. I put my gun down and caught the hog but didn't have a tie rope.

Skeeter was hollering, "Suey!" but my dogs weren't going with him a-hollering. They had all come back to me. When Skeeter came around with a tie rope and took the hog, I took my dogs and went on. I heard Skeeter's four-wheeler take off wide open, but that's just the way Skeeter and little Hersh drive. In a little while he came driving up behind me. I could see that the metal rack over the front tire looked bent down and the front fender was flopping like a broken wing.

I said, "What happened to you?"

He said, "My bulldog had a wreck," and laughed.

"It was bound to happen riding with you."

"That wasn't the way it happened." He had tied the bulldog with a double snap. One end was snapped to the bulldog, and the other end snapped into a tie rope that was left wrapped around the handlebars of the four-wheeler. Skeeter had left his four-wheeler running when he took over the hog, and I had left with my dogs. The bulldog had jumped off the four-wheeler when the tie rope that was wrapped around the handlebar caught the gas lever, pulling it back and causing it to be wide open. When the four-wheeler took off, the bulldog sat back on the tie rope, and that turned the handlebars into a circle, causing the four-wheeler to make two rounds before it laid onto its side.

I said, "A wreck you can walk away from is a good one."

A week or so later, Skeeter and I were together again when we got into some fat shoats that weighed close to one hundred pounds each. I'd caught the one the dogs had caught as Skeet laid to them with his rifle. After the dogs left me, they ran one hog into another place. Skeeter was in pursuit, going to a gap and then back across a branch that he'd crossed a lot of times; however, beavers had dammed up this branch, and there was a lot of water covering over this ground. He missed the crossing by a few feet and went off the bank, drowning his four-wheeler.

I had gotten my hog into the water and tied to a bush when I barely could hear him hollering. When I got there, he was standing in water and had broken the beaver's dam, causing the water level to lower. When I got around to his four-wheeler, the back end and tail light were all I could see.

Everyone's not so fortunate as to walk away from a wreck. There will come a time when we all will give an account. Be wise! Seek God's will and be quick to agree with God. Do business God's way; don't just walk away.

LEFT: Hunter Taylor, 11, of Bedias, seals a deal with a handshake with cowboy author Lloyd Perry, of Singleton. Perry was showing his most recently published book, "A Lasting Impression: Cowboying Around," at the Writers' Guild's book signing at the Truman Kimbro Center in Madisonville on Feb. 20.

OL' PORKEY
TRYING TIMES

*L*ife can be a roller-coaster ride sometimes for both the human and the beast of burden. Here are a few things that I've learned over the years in trying to make the trip. It's important to go back to the normal, basic, fundamental practice of correctly starting a horse. I like to use a round pen. While circling, give a cue and make a small circle several times. Pay attention to what the horse cues off of. After an hour of warming up, make sure he's got room, but try turning into the fence for a walking roll. Pay attention to cue and how he places his back feet. I don't do many rolls, and not any until the horse is warmed up. If there is a problem and he's not setting his feet properly, I usually go to the middle of my pen and make him back up a few times. I then back a couple of steps and roll each way then spend more time in circles. This is where I work on my leg cues. I expect response from my cue and a little neck rein. The longer we circle, the more I drive the point home.

Now, you can tell a cowboy, but you can't tell him much. On the other hand, most cowboys won't tell too much either. Until now, I never told that I did the basics over again and depended mostly upon outside help. I've always just said, "God, help me turn things around."

In the spring of 1996, I'd bought a horse for $1500. At the time it was $1000 more than what he would have weighed over the scales yet $1000 less than he'd cost as a year-old weanling off the mare. He'd been broke and then ridden before being taken to the roping pen and started as a calf horse. He began showing potential, able to run up then stick his back end in the ground and slide an eleven. He'd gotten the attention of some folks with extremely big bucks that buy potential calf horses.

Now, they tell me, right out of the clear blue, this old pony "blew." They didn't know if it was the pressure or if it was his chemistry that got out of whack. All of a sudden, he became untrained. He would no longer stop as before; instead, he'd run away, passing the calf, and would not stop. After seven different horsemen all tried working this old pony through this problem, I never knew what the analysis may have been. I think I'm safe in saying it was a unanimous decision that this old pony had "blown it." I personally believe that if this old pony had not gotten extremely hard riding by Luther the last four to six months before I bought him, it's possible that instead of a sour calf horse, he could have been a spoiled idiot.

After having bought this old pony, we had a couple of days of bad weather. I took this old pony to my round pen and did the ABCs of any horseman. I decided that somewhere in this old pony's past, he'd had some good riding and correct teaching. I was surprised this old pony didn't know how to side path. We began working on a side path right and left. We took a few shortcuts and had this old pony riding around extremely well.

Luther and I were hunting four to six days a week, catching and selling hogs. Some of my days were pretty long, and it showed on me, my dogs, and this old pony.

Whenever I'd get a day job, I'd ride old Easter. It was months before I had a chance to set this old pony up on a cow. I'd heard that he would not cow, and true to the word, he wouldn't pay a cow any attention. When this gentle cow would move, I'd make it a point that we'd move. When she'd stop, we'd stop. We worried this old cow for a long time when she decided she'd had enough of this nonsense and would go back to the herd. I turned this old pony's head and cued him for a side path, but he must have forgotten the ABC's. When I spurred him up, we overtook her in a side path. I let him go past her before pulling him up and getting him started toward heading her. This time the cow cut back hard, and he kept going in a side path. I couldn't pull him up, and we went right into a burnt pine tree top. Those limbs were whipping, popping, and breaking upon us both. How he managed to stand up was a miracle.

Until now I had a pretty good Watergate case. I'm ashamed to tell how I failed God. This old pony didn't have anything on me; I'd blown it too. I thank God for the forgiveness of sin. Now, it was against my will to quit this old pony, but I knew you can't train mad. You'll untrain. I believe that God is concerned about every mite detail of life. God wants to be part of all we say and do. We hunted hard several days, and then I had a day job and rode Ol' Porkey. This old pony did okay. He was a good-looking horse, and we continued practicing riding around every chance we got.

I finally got an opportunity to set this old pony up on another cow. This cow wasn't as gentle as the first old cow. She moved and stopped a couple of times, and I felt his response. She tried us hard a third time. As I pulled him up and quit her, I felt him tremble, making me think, *He's thought of those bridle rings (over and under).* So I eased my hand up on his neck and spoke gently. We eased back into that bunch of cows, worked another one, and quit on a good note. We had a few more practice sessions. From that day since, this old pony and me have come a-riding, giving God credit and glory for turning our roller-coaster way of life around.

Now, Mr. Bill Bay, whom I bought this old pony from, started calling him "Porkey," for he was beginning to gain a name as a hog-hunting horse. However, I had no idea that one day "Old Porkey" would be one of the few isers that I've ridden.

I'd gotten acquainted at Bedias Baptist Church with a young man, Mr. Hunter Taylor, who is twelve years old and competes in the Texas Youth Ranch Rodeo Association. In 2010 at a book signing, Hunter bought a copy of my first book, *A Lasting Impression: Cowboying Around.* That summer Hunter began hunting hogs with me and would ride Ol' Porkey, who is now eighteen years old. In the fall, Hunter's ranch rodeo horse came up crippled, and I offered Hunter the use of Ol' Porkey, if he thought they'd be able to get along. Having made the full circle in life, Ol' Porkey is once again performing well in an arena for Hunter, who is learning to spend time alone in prayer. Praise God.

LIVING A DREAM

$\mathcal{G}$rowing up, I had never given thought to choosing some kind of career for life. It wasn't hard to see that my plans were different from the other folks that I knew. My occupation in life didn't paint a very bright future in the minds of most folks, especially my mom and dad.

Mom and Dad were concerned about how I planned to live this carefree way of life and would ask, "How are you going to pay your bills?" That was a hard question that I'd spent time pondering on for countless hours while sitting on my hip pockets with a good horse between my knees. I didn't have the answers to the future.

So I'd say, "If you don't make bills, you don't owe 'em," or, "I'll hold 'em to a minimum and take cowboy wages and day work 'em off."

I knew my folks knew about living a hard lifestyle. They had lived and worked through together what I have always considered a good life. But they were concerned that I might crop out a failure. I've always come across that I didn't want to take nobody's wages except cowboy wages. I would do enough to keep the wolf away from the door. My work ethics weren't very good. I'd loaf while cowboying around. Then I'd spend the midnight oil trying to make things pan out, saying, "I'd rather work smarter than harder."

Only a few men, and not one single woman that I have ever known, have ever said to me, "You're living what others only dream about." To live a cowboy's life is good, but in reality living a Christian cowboy life is the best.

THE MAN FROM THE NAVASOTA RIVER

It was back in the early 1990s. Mr. James Altamore was feeding a good many slop hogs over on Panther Creek. Now, Panther Creek heads back to the north toward the old Johnson Ranch and flows south into the Navasota River. Toward the west of Panther Creek there are some sand hills that are covered with thick yaupon brush that break off into the Navasota River bottom. Both the creek and the river are flowing southward about a half a mile apart.

Wild hogs, but more especially the boars, are known for breaking into hog pastures. In the 1990s there didn't seem to be as many hogs or humans in the country as there are today.

From the hog pen, west across Panther Creek, there was a fairly large tract of land that's thick brush-covered from fence to fence. On the far west side of this place, across a deep, dry gully, is a small thicket inside a large thicket. The small thicket is as thick as it gets. I don't believe you could drive a butcher knife into it with a sledgehammer.

In 1992 there were four or five Perrys hunting on Panther Creek. When the dogs bayed to the west, just inside this thick tract of land,

Mr. Scott Perry was allowed the privilege to shoot this extremely large boar hog. He was using some kind of big deer rifle with a big scope. Now, when the hog ran, I was for cutting off his shirttail. His uncle Hershel said that he'd hit the hog, but the bullet must have hit that hog's shield (thick, tough shield on the hog's neck and front shoulders).

About five minutes after Scott shot, the dogs all hushed. They were looking for a blood trail, but some of us went on toward the dogs. When we got to that deep gully where the little, thick thicket begins, we began to gather dogs.

It was a couple of years later that Hershel, Hershel Jr., Mr. Howard Slone, and I bayed up a hog in that bad little thicket. I'd crossed this gully and had crawled thirty or forty yards. I came upon the remains of a big hog. The top and bottom of the skull were still together. So I took a pigging string (tie rope) and gathered it up, knowing it would be hard to carry but that I might never be back and that it wouldn't be easy to find if I did come back. I had no idea this skull would be so much trouble as I wormed my way through this thick brush.

I was fairly close to this hog the dogs had bayed when he pulled freight out toward the northwest. I wasn't sure which way would be the best way out. So I hollered at Hersh, who was a short piece from me, and said, "Let's go to the Johnson Ranch."

He said, "How's the best way out of here?"

I said, "Try the shortest, for there ain't no good way out or in."

We finally made it out of that thicket and found Hershel and Howard waiting on us, so I told 'em about this skull and the remains of this hog that had gone into this thicket and must have gotten stuck in there. He probably couldn't go any farther forward, and he couldn't back up and just died in there.

Hershel said, "You know that Scott's hog."

"Scott's, my hind foot. I'm the one who hung up and liked to have died in there getting it out. Furthermore, it probably wouldn't mean nothing to him."

We'd gone a long ways up the river. We knew we were going to have to cross over and go west to find our dogs. We finally found some logs among a bunch of drift and thought we might be able to walk two logs and get across.

Hershel thought Hersh and me ought to cross over the river, go kill the hog, and catch the dogs. When we got back, they would have dinner cooked. Now, it didn't sound that bad. At least it was a plan. Only thing, I was wagging that hog skull. Hershel said that he'd pack it back to the truck for me.

Hersh and I walked these logs without falling in or getting wet. We headed west until we came out of the bottom, crossed over some hay fields, and then an old oil field road. We'd heard our dogs for a while, but when we got to this road, we could tell these dogs were on a long slue (hole of water). We didn't want to walk to the south 'cause we'd be seen from off this road, so we both started up the other side of this slue. But the hog crossed over, and I went back and was walking toward the dogs to the south in the opening.

I heard a vehicle coming, but I couldn't go nowhere. A man and a woman in a double-seated truck drove up. As I was walking back toward them, this big fellow got out, and I said, "Howdy!"

He never said, "Howdy," but began asking a lot of questions.

I noticed the lady and said, "Howdy, ma'am!"

She smiled and said, "How are you?"

"Not so good at the present, ma'am."

The man stood there all mad-like and said, "You going to answer me, or do I go get the law?"

I said, "Sir, I'm not trying to be smart, for I imagine that you're the landowner. Where I'm from, we're a little more neighborly. We speak, and then we start asking questions. I'm a Perry, and we followed that hog and our dogs over here from Panther Creek off Altamore's place in Grimes County."

The man said, "You got somebody with you. Call him out here."

"He's another Perry, my nephew. He'll be here as soon as he kills that hog and gets those dogs."

"Call 'em on that radio. Tell 'em don't kill that hog. Catch them dogs and get up here. Now!"

"Mister, he can't do that, short of killing the hog."

"You gone crazy? Are you gonna to tell 'em?"

I said, "Hersh! This dude said, 'Don't kill that hog. Catch them dogs and get up here.'"

About that time, Hersh's .30 went off. The man said, "What in the world is wrong with y'all? Can't he understand English?"

About that time Hersh came on the radio and said, "What did you say?"

I said, "I think you just blew it. Now get the dogs and get up here."

While we were waiting on Hersh, this fellow had gotten over some of his mad and asked, "Where did you say that y'all came from?"

"Altamore's, on Panther Creek."

"Do you know how far that is?"

"I'm afraid I do."

When Hersh walked up, this fellow stuck out his hand and said, "I'm Morgan Cook." They shook hands.

Then Hersh said, "Mr. Cook, I went to school at A&M, and I know your grandson Aubrey Cook."

Mr. Cook said, "Boys, you'll tie your dogs in the back of the truck. I'll take y'all back around there, for I want to see y'all's truck. It's hard for me to believe y'all would follow those dogs and a hog that far." When we got back to our truck, Hershel and Howard had sausage cooking over a wire mesh in a hole dug out in the ground. Hershel invited Mr. and Mrs. Cook to lunch. They declined the offer and said, "That's a good six miles as the crow flies. I just wanted to see if y'all really came that far."

Lloyd Perry
Singleton, Texas

MY HOG

About 1994, I was roughing it, for times were rough back here in the Old West. I was experiencing the worst crisis of my life, when adding insult to injury the motor in my '89 GMC truck gave up. I didn't have the money to have it fixed; I just sold the old truck and either went horseback or afoot. I was tired of old trucks and had my sights set on a new Dodge diesel for quite a while. It didn't make any difference about the color, as long as it was red. It was a long hard go, trying to gather that $25,000 in order to buy that truck.

When I failed to show up for church in Bedias that first Sunday morning after my truck had given up, that afternoon Mr. and Mrs. Billy Ford came checking up on me. They provided me with transportation back and forth to church for a couple of weeks. Another couple in our church had bought a new car. They offered me the loan of their old car. Now, I was hesitant about using this car and was humbled that they offered me the loan of it. So I smiled and said, "Thanks, but I had better not."

They asked me, "Why?"

"I'm not much on borrowing, and furthermore things could happen."

They assured me it wasn't a big deal, that they only wanted to help me, and the old car was up in shape. This lady said it wouldn't hurt it if I hauled my dogs or a hog in it. So I paid for the insurance and paid for all the upkeep, and I was back in a ride.

I couldn't believe I was sporting a touring car (an Oldsmobile Monte Carlo) that I soon named "Old Helen." Now, I have no idea what all the folks were thinking or saying about this rig and me. When my old dogs and me rolled into somebody's town, we raised a few eyebrows. Some people would be smiling, pointing, or waving. The trunk lid was opened up so that my old dogs could get plenty air, and a lot of the times, along one side of the trunk, a big hog would be laid in there with its head hung over the turtle hull plum down to the bumper.

Now, "Old Helen" was a faithful old car that served me well over a year. It's always been my way to be early if I had someplace to be. If I ever missed any church, it wasn't that old car's fault. I'd get a thirty-minute jump on the rest of the churchmen, and I'd make coffee. I'd make that first pot of coffee to my own liking, for it don't take much water to make good coffee.

There was an old rancher who'd be the first to follow along after I got the coffee made. We'd go back to his classroom and visit. If he had a hog problem, I'd go over and put a stop to it. One time, right out of the clear blue, he handed me a hundred-dollar bill and said, "Buy the car some gas and the dogs a little dog feed." I thanked him, for I had been experiencing some hard times trying to pay all my bills.

Now, one Sunday morning this old rancher no-showed, so I moseyed back down to our classroom and was reading my Bible when three ladies came into the room. They were talking about someone who had died in their sleep.

This one lady said, "That would be such a pleasant way to expire."

Now, I didn't mean to draw any attention, but the way she put it struck me odd, and I lightly snickered. It wasn't a good laugh like some folks do, and I probably would have been overlooked as a dumb, ignorant cowboy by a couple of these ladies.

But this one lady had to make an issue of my snickering by say-ing, "And what do you think, Mr. Perry?"

I looked up from where I was reading, knowing that I should have done the right thing and apologized for snickering and just let it go. But (*but* has gotten me into a lot of trouble), all three of them had their eyes zeroed in on me, and being a pretty good Texas cowboy, I never wanted to disappoint anyone by them not believing that I wasn't something from way out West.

So taking all this in, finally I said, "About what?"

"Dying."

"We all will, unless the LORD comes."

"That's not what I meant, and you know it."

I knew I oughta done what was right, but I'm afraid I done kind of bad, and that instance I knew what I was going to say. "Unless we take things into our own hands, this matter of how we die ain't actually up to us. But if I had my rathers, when it comes my time, I hope I'm alone in the woods, my dogs have a big hog bayed up, and that old hog just eats me up."

I noticed two of these ladies made the ugliest faces you ever saw on a woman. They put their hands over their mouths, saying, "O-o-oh, yuck!" and left in a hurry. But when I looked around, Helen was just standing there with her hands on her hips, a sour smile on her face, shaking her head, saying, "You won't do!"

Now here's the rest of the story: you can't run, nor hide, from the integrity of your character. It wasn't but twenty-four hours later that my old dogs had a big hog bayed in a berry briar thicket that was full-grown. Sometimes nothing is simple and easy, for what should have been a walk in the park was now the basis for crawl-ing to getting in close. Survival experience will teach you to have the wind in your face, for hogs have a keen sense of smell. Another thing is to be quiet; therefore, I looked for a hog highway (trail), for this action was going to be to get down on your belly with the gun out front and belly crawl.

Now, I'd been crawling down this hog highway for what seemed like a mighty long ways when I had a flash: *What if this is my hog?* I stopped, got up on my knees, and got to the ready, for I knew I was close to that sucker, but I just couldn't see very far out in front of me. So I found a window where I could see the best, where I thought this hog would be, and tried to settle down as I told myself, *This ain't no time to be thinking about stuff like that. I was funning, that's all, just being smart.*

Now, that kind of thinking could cause you to make a bad shot, mess up, and just spoil this sport for good. I saw movement as this hog made a dash at a dog, and through this window as he was coming back to his bed, this big sucker filled up that little space as I touched off the trigger of this gun and fired my shot. Now, that old hog's head, along with nearly sixty more, adorns the top of my cabinets along the north wall of my home. They don't mean a thing to any normal humans and don't impress nobody but another cowboy who shared in similar experiences of a real blood-pumping high. I find myself looking more and more at these old trinkets (hog heads, domino trophies, and drawings) that I've collected as I feel the days and years slipping away. I've trained on a few horses and dogs and feel the effects of becoming an old-time cowboy.

In the fall of 1995 I was fortunate enough that I managed to get enough money to buy a new red 1996 Dodge diesel truck. I also bought "Old Helen" and gave her to my daughter Lynn, for something had happened to her ride. She drove the car about a year, got something else, and wanted to know what I wanted to do with "Old Helen." We knew an evangelist soul-winning Indian preacher named Phillip Wade. I don't know what all Lynn told him when she asked if he could use this car, but Lynn said Mr. Phillip laughed and said, "It won't be long before 'Old Helen' will look like a real Indian car, with oil leaks and baloney wrappers thrown all over the floorboard."

I checked on Phillip and "Old Helen" about a year later, and they both were doing fine. The next time I checked, Phillip was in the nursing home. He had diabetes for a long time. Later they got me word that Phillip had passed away.

I visited three of the churches that Phillip had a part in starting that were made up of transformed drunken Indians. Phillip witnessed one-on-one and won them to the LORD Jesus Christ as these drunken Indians were turned out of jail on Monday mornings. Phillip would feed them breakfast as he talked to them about the LORD Jesus Christ. By sharing his testimony, he'd won a lot of the men and their families to Christ. Then he'd start a Bible study, and later on there would be enough to start a cottage prayer meeting in someone's garage. Then after a while they would build a church. Strange, we want to build them a building with our money but are unwilling to go into the field ourselves.

RIGHT OUT OF THE CLEAR BLUE

$\mathscr{B}$ack in 1997, the year started out being pretty trying. Wild hog prices had bottomed out, after having come off an exceptionally good year in 1996. Now, my old hog-hunting pard had shanghaied me, and I was left looking at my options when I had this flash.

These weekend warriors had made a fad out of hog hunting. This was the way they entertained themselves after a forty or maybe fifty-hour week on somebody else's clock. They'd bunch up from five to seven in a group, and maybe twice that many dogs, and go somewhere and catch a wild boar.

Keeping a low profile, I didn't know any of these sports fans. But I'd heard of a few folks that had been offered a lot of money for a good dog. It made sense to me that these people working forty to fifty hours a week would not have time to train a dog. The way I train, it takes me a year to a year and a half, hunting a dog two, three, and sometimes four times a week. It also made sense to me; if they're making twenty-five to fifty dollars an hour, they'd have money to compensate a man for his time invested in training.

I first had to deal with a couple of factors. Fact number one was that success in training wasn't any guaranteed deal. Fact number two was that I couldn't train but one dog at a time, but I could be starting two more. Fact number three is that some folks don't want to give you a pup you're going to sell as a trained dog. So I began to try to stay within my own boundary, using my own dogs.

Being blessed with one or two dogs that carry my trademark (being a one-man dog), it really wasn't me that had anything to do with the training, except that I was faithful to practice 'em. In itself, practicing 'em doesn't account for much. There are some dogs that you can practice every day and they don't make it. Breeding in dogs plays a major role. Some are littermates that you practice three or four times a week. One dog may make it, and the other one don't. So, if breeding and practice aren't the answer, then there is one other factor in this equation: you're blessed. If you are able to realize that, then you're able to realize it's for God's glory. God placed a blessing in your hand for the purpose of crediting him all the glory, praise, and honor.

In 1997 I sold two of my three dogs for large amounts of money to weekend warriors. This was the opening of what I called "running a high-price shop."

In 1998 I had four dogs: Ol' Bunt, Ol' Lou II, and two no-name black gyps. The first two dogs I named were keepers (one-man dogs), but I was experiencing a lot of problems with the two black gyps. One was extremely fast but didn't want to stay hooked (bayed). She'd quit a bay and go hunt another hog. That will mess up your pack if left unattended. The other black gyp was a lot slower and didn't have the capability of the first, though they were littermates.

Up until 1999 I'd hunted the old-time way of listening and coursing my dogs as they ran a hog out of hearing. I'd go in the direction that my dogs went, listening for the dog and looking for hog tracks, especially if they crossed a dirt road. If I could find these tracks, I was able then to get on line, and I ain't talking about a computer. What a cowboy knows ain't much more than what a hog or cow knows, only they know that when a big hog pulls out, he's got someplace definite in mind that he intends to go. You're blessed if you have a dog that can run up and hit (bite the hog's back end) and make him spin around and bay. This will stop the hog from running two or four or maybe six miles before he gets to his destination. Then after he gets there, he may decide to move on the dogs, usually in a trot. This kind of hog will check your oil and separate out all the true hunters and the real hog dogs. After six to ten hours of this, it's easy to tell one form the other, as they fall by the wayside.

I sold Ol' Bunt that would hit a hog, and now I didn't have a dog that would hit, so I decided in 1998 to invest in some of this modern technology and bought a tracking system for eight hundred fifty dollars cash. It was only a short time after I purchased this tracker that I was showing a dog to a good weekend warrior, Brandon Penton of Cleveland, Texas. We had gotten a bay, but the hog broke, running out to the southeast toward Hopewell. On account of a lot of rain, south Bedias Creek was full banked, and we left my four-wheeler at the creek and crossed over on a log. We were foot-backing it, using this tracker to follow my dogs. We'd gone over a mile through the woods, crossed a fence, and had come across a branch into an open hay field. There at the edge of a branch next to some trees stood two young buck deer, one four-point and a six-point. Surprisingly, they didn't run as we walked right up close to these deer. We kept walking up to the deer until we both put our hands on the four point buck's head and horn.

That's very unusual, to be miles and miles from nowhere and out of the clear blue run into a pet buck deer in the woods. Penton had asked me to be sure to write this story, for he had said he has told several people and nobody would believe him.

WORK IT OUT

It took a real miracle for me to graduate from high school in 1963.

I was driving a 1959 Thunderbird, my rodeo car, and I'd missed a lot of day-working cattle and hauling because of not having a rig. I said something to my banker, for I'd borrowed a little money on just my name. He suggested I have Dad's signature on this note; however, when I talked to Dad, he asked me how much money I had. I had nearly nine hundred dollars and needed to borrow one thousand dollars more in order to buy a new 1963 Chevrolet truck.

Dad asked, "Have you ever considered feeding hogs?"

I said, "No, sir."

"Feeding tankage; it's work, but it's the cheapest way."

After I told him that I only had a little money and wasn't interested in going broke in the hog business, he said, "Then I'm afraid I won't be able to help you. You'll have to work it out." I got mad and wouldn't talk to Dad, but it didn't seem to bother him too much.

After about a month of this cold treatment, one night at the supper table Dad said to Mom, "Ask our son what he's going to be doing tomorrow."

Mom said, "I will not. If you two don't cut this out, I'm going to quit cooking for either of you."

Dad said to me, "I need you to help me in the morning."

I nodded my head. Later I asked Mom, "Why won't Dad sign my note?"

She came back with, "Why wouldn't you listen to him?" You couldn't side these two against the other. I came around in November to Dad's way of thinking and said, "I'm ready to go broke buying some cheap hogs or else make enough to buy a new truck."

All Dad said was, "Good! Take to 'em." I bought twenty head of good, white shoats that weighed approximately eighty-five pounds that cost fifteen dollars a head.

Dad only said, "Those are good hogs, but buy them smaller, for these will be ready before June gets here. You want to sell on a June market."

I bought thirty-three head more from nine to twelve dollars each, a ton of milo for the hog feeder, and had a little over one hundred dollars left in the bank.

Dad smiled and said, "You're in business."

I nodded my head in a way that if it would have fallen off I would have never caught it and then said, "What a deal."

I was going to school, but Dad made me keep tabs on the market. Top hogs were bringing eighteen to twenty dollars per hundredweight. By the end of January, those first twenty white shoats had done good.

As Dad looked at them with me one evening, he said, "Do you know the market?"

I said, "Around twenty-five to twenty-six cents a pound for top hogs." I sold the twenty white hogs the first of February and had enough to order and pay for my new truck, for I had sold a few calves also to make up the difference.

By June hogs hit thirty-five cents a pound, the highest they'd been in a few years. I sold out of the hog business and bought a new truck and a sixteen-foot gooseneck trailer with money left in the bank for whatever kind of cow deal that I thought I could get into.

COUNTRY HOG BUYER

Over the years I've worn a good many different hats in the line of work I'm in. I've caught and sold a good many old hogs; however, there comes a time in life when you can't do what you used to and you start pulling up and watching these young hands put on a good show.

It's not hard to admit you can't do what you used to whenever so many body parts hurt after a hard day. I began telling myself a lot of old-time worn-out cowboys had to turn cook in years past in order to eat. The more I thought about that, I figured that I better keep looking for something else and hope that something turned up, for I'd never make it as a cook.

Now, it's hard to get ahead of these young hands, for they don't miss much. If over the years you've earned their respect, you will graduate to a riding job right before you get the gate (expired). Most old-time cowboys have thought of this and have some strategy as to how they'll try to keep the wolf away from their door.

I've been blessed with a little land, a few cows, and a few yearlings that I've always been able to fall back upon. I still enjoy the riding and the training of horses and dogs, but that's only a matter of time. It's hard to put in all the hours that are required of you when you have to go with the horse and dogs. So when a young hand named Skeeter thought I'd make a good hog buyer and told Mr. and Mrs. Tarver they might ought to visit with me, I pondered the deal over in my mind and thought he might be on to something. If it wasn't for all the paperwork, the job wouldn't be half bad.

I set my own working hours. Catch me by phone if you can, or call at night and come the next morning. I know that I'll never get rich as a country hog buyer, but it might be a way in which I can be used by God to finish living out what I profess in Christ Jesus.

Now, my old pard, Luther, was the first to do business at my new hog-buying station. He brought me five good hogs. Three more hunters and trappers all stopped for the grand opening of the Singleton Country Hog-Buying Station just for a visit and to socialize.

BIG LAKE CREEK HOG

I was cowboying around one cold afternoon in November of the 1970s. It was deer season, and there was a cold, stiff, north wind blowing. I wasn't doing anything important, and I kind of hoped to run into some old-timers sittin' around in Roans Prairie or Shiro, Texas. I don't know of anything I'd enjoyed more than listening to some old-time tale of long ago. After speaking and shaking a few hands, this one fellow motioned for me to come over to where he was.

The fellow asked, "Do you still buy cattle range delivered?"

Now, that kind of question is the kind that usually gets my most undivided attention. With a smile I said, "That depends. It's deer season, and we're headed into winter. I'd rather buy 'em next spring."

The fellow began by saying, "I don't know all the details, but I'll tell you what I know. I'll give you a name and directions on how to get there. If you're interested, you can do the rest. It'll be up to you." I found something for him to write directions on. As he finished he said, "This is an old widow woman. Her cattle range up and down Lake Creek. Her son trapped part of the yearlings. Then they got somebody with some horses that had scattered these cattle. They

are just now coming home into their home range. That's about all
I can tell you."

I said, "I sure thank you. With nothing much else to do, I think
I might mosey on down into that country and see if that place is
still there."

Upon arriving at this old residence, I walked up on the gallery
and knocked on the front door. When this older lady opened the
door, with my hat in hand, cowboy-style, I said, "Ma'am, I'm Lloyd
Perry from Singleton. I was told you had a few yearlings you were
wanting to sell."

She made me repeat my name and where I was from. After
repeating my name I said, "I was told you had a few yearlings for
sale."

She said, "Oh, yes, but I have no way of penning them."

"Sometimes I buy cattle range delivered, but with it being deer
season and winter coming on, I'll either catch your yearlings for you
by the head or else wait until next spring to buy them."

"Mr. Perry, how much are you willing to pay per head?"

"Ma'am, I have to see your stock. I normally catch 'em for
twenty-five dollars a head. Now, I normally try to buy for fifty dollars less than what they'll bring at the auction sale. This roping and
choking, you're apt to kill something real easy. I have to buy 'em
cheap enough that if I kill one, I can still make a little money. If
I'm catching 'em for you and I kill one, I don't make the twenty-
five dollars for catching it, but I don't lose the one hundred or one
hundred twenty-five dollars the yearling is worth. Does that make
any sense to you?"

"Yes. Now, if you'll go to the back of the house, out past the
barn, you'll see an old wagon road that'll lead you to the bottom
field. The cattle are usually in this field."

When I walked past the old crib and barn, all the doors were
left open. I noticed that she didn't have any hay. I found the wagon
road and hadn't traveled too far until I came to a little branch with
some big rocks that were probably hauled in from somewhere else

in a wagon. While crossing this branch, I noticed a big, lone hog track that came into this road. The closer I got to this bottom field, I noticed a lot of old rooting and then some made the night before. I noticed the cattle as they ran, and it looked like maybe six or eight head of four hundred-pound yearlings at twenty-five to thirty-five cents per pound or one hundred to one hundred forty dollars per head. For some reason, those yearlings didn't concern me near so much as that hog.

When I got back, the lady had me come into the house by the fire. I said, "Ma'am, I seen six or eight of your yearlings. They are worth an average of one hundred twenty dollars per head at the sale barn. I also noticed you don't have any hay."

She said, "Nope, they'll have to make it on a few cubes and switch cane."

"Those yearlings don't know anything about eating a cube. Get your son to buy you twenty-five square bales of hay. Scatter two bales around in your pen every morning and then call those cattle up as you go to the house. I think those yearlings will eat hay, and you can trap 'em after feeding a week or ten days. If it don't work, then I'll try to buy 'em or catch 'em for you. There's also a big hog down there. Did you know about it?"

"Yes, but none of my neighbors are missing a hog. It's doing a lot of rooting. Can you catch a hog?"

I smiled and said, "I believe I can."

"You're welcome to the hog, but I can't pay you for catching it."

"That's fine, ma'am. I'll get the hog the first chance I get." I thanked her and said, "I'll be back this evening or tomorrow and stop that hog from rooting."

Now, I left there about 3:30 p.m., but I couldn't get that big hog off my mind. I went home and got my two dogs, Ol' Mitzie and Ol' Junior.

At five o'clock I met Pat Arrington where he worked and told him about finding this big hog track and rooting. All he said was, "Let's go!"

We got back to this lady's house about fifteen minutes until six o'clock that evening. I hadn't thought about no light until now. We decided to split up. Ol' Junior would go with him, but Ol' Mitzie had my trademark and wouldn't hunt for anyone but me. She was a one-man dog. In twenty minutes or so, Ol' Mitzie bayed. It was already pretty dark inside that thicket. Not long after Ol' Junior got there, that hog ran at him; I noticed this was an extremely big, fat sow. Ol' Junior had caught her by the ear, and there was a lot of thrashing around in those wild roses.

I tailed this big sow, picking up one rear hind foot. She *wooshed* real big and was taking Ol' Junior and me on into those roses until the brush finally stopped her. We weren't there but a few minutes when Pat got there and got a front foot, and we got her lay on her side. Now, he squalled like a panther. I just ever so lightly gave it that "Hee-hee-hee!" After getting her tied down by all four feet, we put two pigging strings in her mouth. We could only pull her ten or twelve feet and had to stop 'cause she was that heavy.

I said, "I'll tie these two ropes that's in her mouth to a tree and turn her feet loose. Tomorrow I'll come back with my horse and drag her out of here."

Pat said, "I crossed a fresh-cut right-a-way coming to you. I know it's not far, and it has to lead back to that road we came in on."

We drug the hog two more times before he went looking for this right-a-way. He hollered when he found it. The dogs and me went to him. We walked out to the road. I went and got my truck and put my dogs up. We drove back down to where I'd put a bush in this right-a-way and stopped. We both went looking for that hog, but it was so dark that we couldn't find her.

He was aggravated that I didn't bring a light and said, "Well, so much for that!"

I said, "I can find her if you can pull her to the truck."

"Time is running out. If you can find that hog, do it, for I need to go."

I turned Ol' Mitzie loose and said, "Suey!" a couple of times. Finally Ol' Mitzie left me and bayed that tied hog. I was afraid that she wouldn't bay that hog after it was tied. We had our work cut out for us, dragging that fat sow fifty yards. When we got to the truck with the parking lights on, we were both completely given out. I didn't say it, but I was afraid we wouldn't be able to load this hog.

Now, I'm built more like a rope, and I'm not all that strong, but Pat was built like a bull and could flat get down and give a lift. I had seventeen-inch wheels on this three-fourth-ton Ford truck. It was at least three feet up to the inside of the bed. I was up in the bed of the truck lifting and pulling up on this hog's head as he came up with the rest of her. I got her head pulled around and tied so she couldn't get to my dogs. We headed out of there. I didn't slow down until we hit that county road.

I'd already told this lady we'd caught the hog when I'd gotten my truck. I went back later and learned that her son bought the hay and later had trapped all the yearlings. Not a bad trade, a little advice for one of the fattest hogs I'd ever caught. There were no hog-buying stations, and the sale barns deducted the value of the hog immensely, so therefore I smoked the sausage and sugar-cured the hams and bacon.

COMMUNITY HOG

In the 1940s folks voted in stock law. The free-range era had ended in our country. Whereas in times past everyone did their best fencing around their fields to fence stock out, folks were now having to fence to hold all their stock in. In order to hold hogs out or in, hog wire or net wire was used, ranging in different heights, and then a couple or three barbed wires were placed over the top of the net wire.

Almost everyone who lived on small farms kept meat hogs either in a pen or a hog pasture. Some folks would keep an old sow and raise pigs each year. The hog in the pen was fed a little grain, but most of its fill was tankage, dishwater, or slop with rice hulls ground into shorts. The hog would be killed in cold weather so the meat would keep while the meat was being cured.

Hogs running in a hog pasture eat grass or tankage for their fill and were given grain also. In the fall—late September to early November—if there was a good mash crop (acorns), most farmers would want to turn their hogs out to fatten on mash, but folks were leery because so many hogs went missing. Dad told me that a lot more people were killed over hog theft than were hanged as cow or horse thieves because folks were always squabbling over hogs.

What a cowboy knows ain't all that much, but I happen to know this: all animals are territorial, and the strongest dominating family rules a range. Intruders are never welcome and are fought, whipped, and run off by the dominating family, and a very old female runs this family.

Now, it wasn't hard for this old-time cowboy, who has nothing better to do than sit on his hip pockets with a good horse between his knees, to study on things of a sort and make this analysis. A lot of these hogs were being pushed from one territory to another by other hogs and not driven off or killed by a thief. However, when hogs drifted into a range and the mark (identification) wasn't known, folks of a baser (lower sort of class of people) would catch an unknown marked hog and either change the mark or cut the mark out (grubbing the ear next to the head). The hog was then considered as community property or fair game to anyone. The problem with having a community hog in your possession was that if the rightful owner found proof the hog was in your possession, it wasn't easy to prove that you didn't cut that mark out. Back here in the Old West it was either way: you lived or died by the gun. As a kid sitting around listening to grown men spin tales, a man said there was a thief killed when he was caught stealing a hog. One of the ears was cut off and crammed down his throat. He was then laid over the saddle of his horse and tied down, with a note pinned on his shirt that read, "This thief was caught while trying to steal a hog and choked to death while trying to swallow the hog's ear."

HUNDRED-DOLLAR COWBOY

I wasn't quite in my twenties when I first started going over into Montgomery County to the Williams Deer Camp in the Sam Houston National Forest. My first visit over there, I was invited to a fish fry. A couple of rounders and me had caught some catfish on the Navasota River. I knew most of the folks at this shindig, for back then I knew nearly everyone within a twenty to twenty-five-mile radius of Singleton. It was only a few years later that I married a young gal whose folks lived on the edge of the Big Thicket (Sam Houston National Forest).

I began going to church over at Pool's Community Church before I married, and I'd gotten acquainted with a good brush cow-boy, Mr. Billy Williams, who attended Pool's Church. I also knew a couple more brush hands: Mr. J.W. Moriarty (wife's dad) and Jimmy Rex Randall (wife's uncle).

It was during these times when a fellow told me, "Church is all right for old men, women, and children, but not much of a place for a man."

I cocked my hat as I said, "Really?" I had noticed there weren't many men in church. He called it like it was, for there was an element of truth in what this tush hog (rough hand) had told me.

After having ridden this national forest for a few years with these three brush hands, I came to realize there was a lot of this old country. Upon helping my father-in-law work his cattle, I became aware of some wild cattle that belonged to Mr. Burl Ship. These cattle were wild and crazy, and if your dogs got after these Ship cattle, these cattle would pull freight (start running). If you couldn't blow your dogs off with a horn right away, chances were that if the dog didn't come back to where you turned out, you were going to spend time looking for your dogs and probably lose some of them. These old Ship cattle weren't nothing but bad news to a cowboy, especially if you were hog or cow hunting down on the San Jacinto River, where these cattle usually stayed.

Mr. Ship had put a fifty-dollars-a-head bounty for any two- or three-year-old Maverick bull caught and hauled to the Huntsville Sale Barn. Billy Williams, Jimmy Randall, and myself thought we'd try gathering a few of these wild cattle. I remember catching one. We had to drag this bull yearling a long ways, horseback, before we could get 'em to a truck and trailer. After I'd hauled this old Maverick bull to the sale and we had split the fifty dollars three ways, there wasn't no money to be made in this deal. The cattle were a lot more trouble than they were worth.

I'd been day working cattle for twenty-five dollars a day for Mr. J.C. Howard and his son, Jake, ever since I had gotten out of school. They were one of my steady customers when in the early 1980s, the Howards had leased a ranch on the San Jacinto River over near Big Sandy. They had stocked this place with one hundred pair (cow and calf), only to find out that Ship had about twenty to thirty head of cattle that also used this range. The San Jacinto River was the boundary between this ranch and the national forest. It was impossible to keep a fence in this river bottom. Furthermore, a fence never meant anything to a Ship cow if they wanted to go somewhere else.

Now, Jake was beside himself, fretting over what to do with

these Ship cattle. He talked about suing the folks who leased this place to them. He talked about buying Ship's cattle and shooting 'em. He really had his fat in the fire.

I said, "Why don't you pen 'em?"

He came back with, "You know nobody can pen those Ship cattle."

"I can."

"I'd give a hundred dollars just to see it."

"Put your money where your mouth is, and I'll show you."

Jake just laughed and said that would be the way to get rid of them. Jake had run these old Ship cattle out and fixed up the fence between the hill part of this place and the bottom. But when some of the Howards' cattle started following these Ship cattle off into the forest, he must have really gotten worried, for he came back to my house one evening and asked me if I was serious or joking about penning those Ship cattle.

I said, "I'm as serious as a heart attack. And for a hundred, I'll even let you watch."

"That's what I wanted to hear. Now, how are we going to do it?"

"Real easy like."

I was talking about handling, not that it would be that easy to pen these cattle.

Among the other hats I wore, I was also the Powder River Livestock Panel dealer for this area. We loaded all the panels I had, new and old, into and on the sides of my trailer. We had one twelve-foot bow gate and one four-foot bow gate that were tied on the sides of the trailer; all the rest were panels. We left my truck and trailer on the dirt road and went into the pasture in his truck, calling the cattle to the far northeast part of this place, and put out several hundred pounds of cake, feeding them heavy so these cattle would stay put while we came into the ranch on the opposite side of this place and set up all these panels on a road that went into the bottom. Right behind this pasture gate and the fence that separated the hill pasture from the river bottom land, we began setting up these two pens.

I had different length panels. All the new panels were sixty-seven inches tall by sixteen feet or fourteen feet or twelve feet long. The old panels that I always used when day working were seventy-two inches tall by either twelve or sixteen feet long. I put the twelve-foot bow gate where the pasture gate sat and built the biggest pen out of the new sixty-seven-inch tall panels. I put the four-foot bow gate in the very back end of this pen and then built a smaller pen out of the seventy-two-inch panels I had. I took a good, stout pigging string and tied the four-foot bow gate half open so that when they found that hole and poured into the back pen, I could get my hand on that rope and pull that gate shut, or it would hang a cow's side if they started pouring back out.

Now, I admit that I didn't sleep much that night, but I did put away a sizeable amount of coffee. I hate those kinds of nights when it gets on your pillow and won't let you sleep. When I've done my homework and prayed through, I don't know why I couldn't just leave it there and trust God. It hit me that Dad might have been right: there is more to ranching than what is done from the back of a horse. Now, I qualified the statement that I've so often made: "If I'd a thought, I wouldn't have been a cowboy."

After I had already made this deal, I had an afterthought. I had been day working for twenty-five dollars a day, Ship was paying fifty dollars a head for these bull yearlings, and Jake was talking in terms of several thousands of dollars for shooting all these cattle. All that an ignorant twenty-five-dollars-a-day cowboy could see was the opportunity to make an easy hundred-dollar bill. I had let over a thousand dollars slip right through my hands.

I remember counting roughly ten of those Maverick bulls when we fed those cattle, and that didn't ring a bell. If Ship was still paying the fifty dollars a head, I ought to have been working for Ship instead of Jake.

I laughed and told Jake. He said, "I'm sorry, but I've made a deal with Ship."

In humor, I said, "An ignorant cowboy don't know nothing about making money."

It was barely breaking day when we pulled inside that old ranch's front gate and unloaded our horses. I had brought only one dog, my old faithful standby, Ol' Mitzie. I told Jake that if he was going to pay me one hundred dollars to see this, he was to stay with me and not say or do anything, just watch or else stay at the truck. He came back with a, "What if?"

I said, "Don't worry. I'll be loading panels. You'll be fixing fence."

When we got over into the pasture about a half mile, I sent Ol' Mitzie. It was just getting light enough to see when Ol' Mitzie started baying.

I hoped it wasn't a hog, but it really didn't matter. I figured those Ship cows would come up off of their bedding ground and start slipping out of that place. All these cattle were used to going out that gate that led into the bottom. I figured all these old cattle were going to pretty much stay with that lead cow out in the front, especially if they didn't see anybody or have any pressure put on them.

I made it to a hill not far into the pasture and waited in the brush as that bunch of cattle was long trotting toward that middle pasture gate and my portable pen. As they got close to the pen, I'm sure that old lead cow may have smelled a rat. But I'd come off that hill running my horse wide open. Those cattle might have heard or seen me and my horse running; all I remember is sliding Ol' Blue up to that twelve-foot bow gate, slamming it, and heading on in the pen for that four-foot bow gate and getting my hands on that pigging string and jerking it closed. I quietly did that hee-hee-hee laugh. I'm sorry to say, but back then I never thought of giving glory to God.

Jake left and went to Ship's house. In about an hour, Ship came with Mr. J.W. Moriarty (Sweet Wib). Sweet Wib hauled two loads of those cattle, I supposed, to the Huntsville Sale Barn, for I never asked what they had planned to do with them.

When Sweet Wib asked me how I managed to pen these cattle, my answer was, "Real easy." I smile, for over the years I've called myself a one hundred-dollar cowboy. No one has ever known what I was talking about, for I was a little ashamed and embarrassed at cheating myself. I don't recollect ever having told the story until now, but I did sell the Howards a lot of Powder River panels afterward!

PAPA PERRY LOOK

*U*ntil now, I have never told anyone about how my dad would pose and how he could give a cool stare when he wasn't pleased with me or anyone else. Now, that got me to wondering how those Perry gals (Lynn, Lee, and Jackie) would know anything about Dad's expression and call it "that Paw Paw Perry look."

I got the job of disciplining and being the bad guy in our family. I never wanted to be any rougher than it took to get my point across. Really never had to get too rough with the girls, but that hammer-headed boy could take a lot before hollering, "Calf rope."

Both Aunt Lynn and Aunt Jackie Ann dearly love little Hopcy. They both love getting little Hope aggravated and will go out of their way to do it. Then they will tell me, "Dad, little Hope is the only one we have ever seen in our family that could make that natural pose and identical expression of Paw Paw Perry's."

Now, that baby is growing up to be a little lady, and those two aunts have finally grown out of being so annoying!

SCAT CAT

*T*his tale was told to me about my youngest granddaughter, Hopey, by her aunt Lynn, who had called early one cold, dark morning before daylight to share all the enjoyment of the early Christmas get-togethers they had and that I'd missed.

After having stumbled to the phone when I heard Lynn's or Jackie's voice, for I can't hardly recognize their voice, all I could think of was "Christmas Eve gift!"

She said, "Dad, it's not Christmas Eve!"

Now, I'm not much of a hand at remembering this old traditional saying, and they all delight in "Gotcha" and "I love you" following it. This tale had its beginnings a few years back when Lynn agreed to let Ashley and Courteney have a kitten. Later on the cat killed a poisonous snake in the yard.

Lynn told me back then, "Dad, I never cared for cats until then."

Now, it seems that their family cat had multiplied, and they brought a couple of cats to their Granny's house the day they had their early Christmas get-together.

They were all busy when Lee saw a cat in the house and asked, "Where did that cat come from? And what's it doing in the house?"

Little Hopey, who was nearby, collected the cat and took it to the door and put it outside while her aunt Lynn was saying that she'd brought the cats and thought they'd be company for her mother. They were good rat cats, and they could be indoor or outdoor cats. I took that to mean if you hollered, "Scat, cat!" you'd better have a hole cut in the door.

Lee said, "You know Mom don't like cats! There'll be cats all over the place!"

"Goodness!" Lynn said. "Two cats don't make Mama's place nothing like Mrs. Murray's!"

After a little while of aggravating, Aunt Lynn sneaked around and let the cat back in the house again. Now when little Hopey realized that the cat was back in the house, Lynn told me, "Dad, there aren't but two people in our family that I have ever seen stand with that Grand Papa Perry expression, with both hands open, with the back of their hands pressed on their hips, elbows straight back, with that Perry look."

Jackie Ann has used that expression, and now little Hopey was standing there with that expression and look when she said, "Now who let that cat in?"

Aunt Lynn said, "I did." Little Hopey collected the cat again and put it outside.

That's how it all got started: little Hopey having a bad hair day, with Aunt Lynn turning those cats in the house. Then Aunt Lynn began picking on Lil Hopey. Lynn would hold her hand like a claw and make a *fitz, fitz* sound. With everyone else laughing, it was enough to drive little Hope crazy if she'd let it! That went on all morning long. When Lynn's bunch all got ready to go home over the mountain from Talihina back to Hartshorne, all the nieces and nephews had kissed her goodbye, except Hopey.

Lynn said, "Come on, Hopey, I've got to go home. Come give me a kiss bye." Hopey just came back with another Perry expression that somehow I knew all too well and said, "Nope."

Lynn said, "Dad, all your grandchildren are so different, but Hopey's hair is dark, streaked with blonde, just like the four Perry girls that you raised!"

PERRY GALS

*N*ow, it had only been four Christmases ago since Aunt Lynn had brought over those two old aggravating cats to her mother's house that Aunt Lynn kept letting into the house. Now after all this time, it looks like most any normal grown person would grow up and cut out all the horseplay. But strange things are happening in the land.

Being as I wasn't there, I put together pieces of the story from three of my daughters, and I believe I can speculate on the rest. It went something like this: Lynn, who lives near McAlester, Oklahoma, must have picked up her mother for a doctor's appointment that previous week. After Lynn and Jackie Ann had taken their mother back to Talihina, they made it to Lee's house while Lee and her bunch were still at church that Sunday evening. So Lynn and Jackie Ann got to clowning around with a couple of Lee's girls' hats and took a picture of themselves with Lee's new camera. Now, I would say it was probably Lynn's idea for them to take the hats. In a few weeks, when they were all to get together at Lee's house for their Christmas get-together (this would be the time when they all would try to put the big pot in the little one), those two old Perry gals were going to come in wearing those Toliver girls' hats.

I suppose that it's hard to break an old habit. As our children were growing up, if anything happened between them and they didn't settle the matter, when one or the other brought word to me, they always stated the other one's full name. Now, as they have grown older and married, if they get disgruntled (and if word get's back to me), they still use one another's full maiden name.

I asked that bunch, "Why is it you'll use my last name when you're fighting?"

They all laughed and said, "We all still enjoy aggravating one another."

That next week when Jackie Ann had taken her mother back to Talihina from the doctor's in McAlester, she took it upon herself to hide Lee's favorite pair of shoes along with her Christmas presents, which had been under the Christmas tree. Now, Jackie Ann's conscience must have got to bothering her, for that night she called Lee. Lee is the head librarian at the Talihina Library and had to work late and had gotten home at dark. She was told that her Christmas presents were gone. She then couldn't find her favorite pair of house shoes, and to top it off, the electrical transformer had just blown up, and they were all now in the dark. When Jackie Ann called, Lee must have had it figured out that Jackie Ann was responsible and gave her the old what-for, making Jackie Ann feel guilty.

Lee said, "This is more like Lynn Perry's doings! I didn't expect something like this from you."

Jackie Ann must have told her that she was sorry that she was in the dark and was in a foul mood. Jackie Ann said that she would call and talk to her dad and talk to Lee again when she was having a better day. Jackie Ann called me and said she just wanted to talk.

Well, I suspected something and asked, "What's wrong?"

She said, "Oh, nothing, Dad, it's just Lee Perry is in a foul mood."

I asked, "What have you and Lynn been up to?"

She laughed and said, "Why do you ask that?"

To answer that question was easy: "I know you two!" But I didn't know that her conscience was bothering her and she was now having doubts about pulling off this hat prank. The truth is, Jackie Ann will slide her horse in there, jump down, and put her hand on a wild hog as fast as I will. So something else was bothering her. She was not scared or showing the white feather (chickening out); however, I didn't have a clue as to what was going on.

A day or two later I called Lee and asked her, "What are those other two gals up to?"

Lee said that she could never tell for sure. If they weren't picking on her, they'd be picking on each other, for with them two, there was never a dull moment.

A week or ten days had passed, and I knew that that Friday evening they would be having their Christmas party at Lee's home in Talihina. I suppose that Jackie Ann had gotten there early, put the hat back, and was now trying to smoke the peace pipe. When Aunt Lynn got there, she was dressed up but had on this kid's hat. Now, those grandkids of ours love Aunt Lynn and are getting old enough to think that she's cool! I don't think Lynn knew whose hat she had on, but she really likes to pick on Little Hopey. When Aunt Lynn came in, carrying food and wearing this new hat, she drew a lot of attention.

When little Hopey saw that hat, she said, "I used to have a hat that looked like that."

One of the other Toliver girls said, "Hopey, that is your hat!"

In disgust, Hopey said, "Well, I'll be!"

THE ONE THAT KEPT
GETTING AWAY

*M*r. William Mellman is an old-time cowboy that I've known for several years. William is a few years older than me, and I am a little older than his brother, Mr. Johnny Mellman. The three of us competed in rodeos in the 1960s and seventies. In our younger years, William was by far the better rodeo hand, and it has a way of showing on him today. William and Johnny are both professional welders. They now both ranch, day work, and hog hunt a good bit. They have a string of good horses and dogs, and they reside over at Hempstead, Texas.

Ever since I moved back to Texas in 1993, wherever William and I happen to run into one another, it is his usual way to say, "Let's go get a cup of coffee. I want to hear a good hog story."

I ain't bad about turning down no coffee. Neither do I try to disappoint anyone with a good hog tale. So I usually come back at him with, "I'd about as soon hear a good tale as I had to tell one."

Since having made it back to Texas in 1993, I've hunted and spent my time alone in the woods with a horse and a dog. It's really been quite a life back here in the Old West. I lived on the edge for a lot of years in my younger life. I must be getting old, for I don't take chances or run the risk that I once took. Anymore, I'm laid-back and content to train on a horse or a dog; therefore, I seldom have a very good story to tell anyone anymore.

William and I had run into each other at the Mid-Tex Sale Barn, and he said, "Let's get a cup of coffee. I want to hear a good hog story." Now, this café gal poured our coffee as a few of the locals began to drag up a chair. I said to Mr. David (Bull) Keyser, who's a rope hand and handy with a hog, "Boy! Prosperity's about stopped you from doing any hunting, hasn't it?"

"No, sir. I went after that good rain the other day."

We were in the hottest part of summer in Texas; it was the last dog days of July. It had been hot and dry, and Bull had caught a big boar hog while helping Flop (Mr. Darrell Burnett). Bull had this old hog in his trailer for several days, when he caught four good sows in a trap. Bull called me to be sure I'd be at the house so I could cut him a check for his pork. I run a hog-buying station.

Bull made a short day in the middle of the week and was going to bring me this swine. But he called back an hour later and said, "Mr. Perry, I ain't coming. All of my hogs are dead."

"Dead? Did you ever hear of watering 'em?"

"Yes, sir, I did, and they still died."

"What about the boar hog in your trailer?"

"All the excitement of trying to load those sows must have killed him, for he's dead too."

"If excitement takes you out, that might be as good of a way to go as any."

After Bull had told about all his hogs dying, everybody was shaking their heads and feeling sorry for him. Well, I hated it too but would have hated it a lot worse if they had all died on me after I had bought and paid for them. I said, "Bull, do you remember that big boar hog we'd seen the first day of hog season last year that stood a foot taller than any other hog in that bunch?"

Bull said, "Yes, sir. We sure caught five head of good hogs that day. One boar hog weighed 230 pounds, and another boar weighed 290 pounds. We'd seen that boar hog with all those other hogs right at dark."

"Yeah, that's the old hog. That's the dominating boar hog that had those Mavericks whooped off. He's a little bigger and whole lot smarter than those other hogs. That hog has put it on me like a real high-brow lady."

William spoke up and said, "What's that! He's put it on you?"

I just smiled and nodded my head up and down like a mule.

"If you want that hog, we'll go get him right now."

I smiled and said, "You don't know how much I appreciate your offer. I guess I ought to take you up on it, for I've had two good shots (loops) at him and missed them both. Little Jim had a throw one morning before we worked the Reeves' cattle and had missed him. Luther, John, and Bo all got thrown out of a three-hour hog race after my dogs had that hog bayed up for two hours. If this old hog don't whack up your pack, then he'd do his best to run you out."

I'd seen this old hog five times this spring and had a run at him two times and missed those two loops. I mostly hunt and train on dogs while riding along sitting on my hip pockets. I thought a lot about this old hog, and he had me doing some thinking. I told William that I'd call this hog Paul Harvey. "If the tides ever change and I am able to ever get him caught, I'll be back with the rest of the story. Good day!" That day came only ten days later.

Lloyd Perry
Singleton, Tex.
8/16/2008

OL' PAUL HARVEY
AND THE REST OF THE STORY

After having told Mr. William Mellman and that bunch of locals about the one that kept getting away and how I was humbled, having missed those two good loops at that hog I called Paul Harvey, I admitted it wasn't a very good tale. But I've found that it's a lot better that I humble myself than for God to do it for me.

It was getting late one Saturday evening one week after I'd told this tale. I wasn't for sure whether it was on purpose or by accident; it could have been the cowboy grapevine that caused Mr. James Ramsey (Skeet) to show up for a visit. It's only once in a blue moon that Skeet's full of talk. I decided it was probably on purpose that he'd shown up like he did. About a month before this, Skeet had Mr. Dusty Winder bring me a plastic dog food sack half-full of hard canning pears. So I went to my food pantry and got a jar of pear preserves and a jar of fig preserves and set them out on the table. I asked, "Do you want these?"

Skeet said, "Yes, sir. You know that I do."

"I must be getting old. I gave William Mellman a couple of jars a while back when he brought a load of hogs. Last Thursday I ran into him at the sale barn. Over a cup of coffee I told a tale on myself that wasn't worth telling."

Skeet laughed and said, "Mr. Perry, what did you tell Mr. Mellman?"

So I told him about the one that kept getting away. Skeet laughed pretty big at me calling that hog Paul Harvey and said, "Mr. Perry, you'll get 'em."

I cocked my head to one side and said, "Really? You think so?"

"Yes, sir."

We talked about our young dogs. He said that he'd been working and hadn't gotten to do much hunting. The last time he went, he'd gone with Mr. Colby Loveal. Colby now had a pretty good pack of dogs.

I didn't know that Skeet would call wanting to go hunting that next Monday morning. I was to show my young dogs, but the fellow who bought Ol' Flip couldn't make it. However, a Mr. Harvey Cannon and a Mr. Chris Williams did show up. We caught five head of hogs, but we didn't find Ol' Paul Harvey.

Mr. Travis Longlum asked me at church that Wednesday night, "Mr. Perry, do you need any riding company?"

I smiled and said, "Come on."

The weather had changed from a hot, dry August to a week of cool, nice, rainy weather. I probably needed a good washing off, for I'd gotten wet a couple of times. Travis rode with me, and we'd put the grub ear (no ears) hog in the lake twice. Each time I was able to stop my dogs and watch that hog swim across the lake.

Hunting conditions were extremely good that next Monday morning after a good rain. My three young gyps took on hog sign on Cat Creek. I never found a hog track and didn't know if we were after a lone hog or family hogs. These gyps had trailed a long ways on both sides of this creek. Finally, they lined out the sign and bayed in a thicket on Bermuda Flat. The hog broke east, and the dogs went with him. I didn't see it, but I credit Ol' Skittey for stopping that hog. He was bayed in some woods and moved into a little grown-up road. I realized that this was Ol' Paul Harvey.

I had my rope down and made a run at him but didn't get a throw. I kept going down this road until I got to an open field, hung a hard left, and would have had an opportunity at a loop as he'd crossed if Ol' Skittey had not hit Ol' Paul Harvey again. Right at the edge of this opening, Ol' Paul Harvey moved back into some thick yaupon brush and decided he'd just wait us out as he fought at my dogs. After about an hour of this waiting game, I moved into this thicket on my horse and fought brush until we were hung up and couldn't go farther forward, backward, or turn around. In disgust, I cut loose with a squall that made all my dogs completely quit barking. I tried to coach 'em back to barking again by clapping my hands, saying, "Suey!"

After about five minutes of begging these dogs to bark, I gave up on them. I figured my dogs thought I was squalling at them and had pulled out. It took me twenty minutes to get out of that thicket. I never heard a dog bark again, so I went to blowing my old goat horn. I didn't know whether those dogs were in the thicket, at the truck, or had left with that hog. They wouldn't come to me when I called them. I thought, *That's about par. I'm beat again.*

I don't know where Travis had gone to, but I rode back west to a hill back toward the TMPA Lake to listen. I said, "Thank you, LORD," for I finally heard the dogs to the south. I had to go the long way around to get to the dogs. As I rode up on this old hog and my dogs, the hog was in a shallow branch lying in some water until he saw me. Ol' Paul Harvey had on a mad and decided to come for me, but Ol' Buck and me moved out of his way and ran toward a little opening leading out of the woods. That led this hog out into the opening, and when Ol' Paul Harvey committed himself to cross this opening, Ol' Buck ran up, and I cast my line at him as he made that little turn. It was not with the finesse I'd seen Skeeter or Cobey rope a hog; however, my rope fell, catching him around the head.

I'd wanted his head and one leg in my loop, but I'd caught him deep (both front legs) up close and right around the middle of his chest.

When the rope tightened up on Ol' Paul Harvey, he was jumping, bucking, and throwing his head up. He cut one strand of my three-strand poly rope, and my eyes bugged out as I saw my rope unraveling. So Ol' Buck and me gave him a good jerking and dragging back toward a tree and got him wrapped around it. Travis finally showed up about the time the excitement was over and caught a hind leg as I stepped off my horse and front-legged him and got 'em tied down. Then I drug that hog back to the same water hole he was laying in earlier. When we got 'em loaded and back to the house, I found Ol' Paul Harvey weighed 252 pounds, making that loop worth $156.20.

I tipped my hat and said, "Thank you, LORD. That's the highest priced loop I've ever made catching anything in all these years."

It was Mr. Paul Harvey's way to say, "Now, that's the rest of the story. Good day!"

OL' SKITTEY
FIFTH EXCEPTIONALLY GOOD TOP DOG

*N*ow, I'd never given much thought as to how some of my old dogs got their names, but Ol' Skittey was an impressive dog. In fact, some of my dogs never got a name until after they were three years old, trained, and sold, and someone else named them. I usually can tell at the yearling puppy stage if they carry my trademark (one-man dogs). If they do, then they may get to stay and eat my gravy train. I use a few basic commands like "Come here!" "Get out!" or "Hey-eee-eee." I like to keep the tone of my voice normal (low) unless I mean business. I don't like to holler, and I don't like being hollered at. A raised voice and rough talk usually lead me to wrath and anger, which only un-trains and is very unprofessional.

Back a few years ago, the hog population wasn't so thick like it is today. I was hunting around in four or five different surrounding counties. I'd been going over in Washington County around Chappell Hill, Texas, down on the Brazos River, for a couple of months in the winter, mostly with my brother Hershel. I noticed that I'd passed up a woman walking in the same area a half-dozen times. This woman walked on the opposite side of the road, always meeting the traffic. When cars were coming from either direction, this ol' gal would back off on the shoulder of the highway near the ditch and watch each car go by. I thought it was kind of strange, so Hershel and I got to calling her Ol' Skittey.

In 2007 Ol' CC whelped a litter of pups. The one I kept is a one-man dog that I called Ol' Skittey. She was athletic and could run up with some of the fastest dogs I ever owned. Being a fast dog doesn't account for much, unless they're able to hit (bite the back end of a hog). This is a time saver and a great help in catching wild hogs for selling alive. This young gyp carried my trademark. She was nervous around people and didn't like strangers and was awful skitty.

The years have taken their toll and slowed me down. I'm not much help, so it seems to these younger hands; however, I'm usually there for the ordeal and to see the show, but that don't really cut the mustard with me. I don't especially like not being able to be a player. It's good to have a contender that's able to make up that little bit of difference that Ol' Skittey mades. I give God the credit, for I have been well blessed.

In July of 2009 I made a trip up into the north country to see Jackie Ann graduate from nursing school. Upon returning home, I found Ol' Skittey had died. A month later Ol' CC (Skittey's mother) got too hot and also died.

OL' SUE BABY II
SIXTH EXCEPTIONALLY GOOD TOP DOG

Along during the Christmas holiday season, the Mellman brothers (William and Johnny) from Hempstead, Texas, cook up a big stew supper and have a real cowboy and rancher get-together. Over the past years, this little gathering has gotten to be a tradition everyone enjoys and looks forward to. Now, I was hauling a four-month-old pup that was born in September of 2008 during the time that Hurricane Ike struck our part of Texas. I called the dog pup Ike, and I named this little gyp puppy Sue Baby II. Ol' Sue Baby II was tied in the back of my truck when I arrived at this shindig.

After shaking everyone's hand, Mr. Johnny Mellman asked me, "What's that you're hauling?"

"A pup out of William's Ol' Ben dog and my Ol' CC Rider gyp." These puppies were not black but a real dark red.

While Johnny and I were visiting, William drove up in his pickup and asked, "What's that Lloyd's got tied in the back of his truck?"

I smiled and said, "That's one of the articles. There's a lot of old has-beens, some could-bes, but very few isers. You may be looking at an upcoming star that may hurt some folks. This pup's name is Sue Baby II."

Now, I was looking at Johnny when I said, "In the past forty-plus years, I've raised a lot of black dogs, but I kept this little red gyp and named her Sue Baby II after William's extremely good top gyp that he called Sue Baby. It was in 1996 when word came to me by the grapevine that a top hand offered William his ride for his gyp called Ol' Sue Baby. William wouldn't trade with this hand, and for the last twelve years I've been trying to raise an extremely good top, red gyp that I could call Sue Baby II and see if this hand was still in the market. I might can't get it done like William, for Mr. Skeeter Ramsey was driving a brand new 2008 Dodge diesel. Nevertheless, I intend on having the goods if Skeet ever decides he wants to make that deal again!"

It was only six months later while William and I were together working some cattle that I was impressed with his young Ike dog; however, I felt Ol' Sue Baby II was a notch above his dog because she was so much faster.

I'm sure William wouldn't admit that; however, he did say, "I've got a truck. I'll trade you for that Sue Baby gyp."

I smiled and said, "All right, I'll trade for that new red Dodge you're driving, but I ain't interested in any old clunker feed truck."

Sue Baby II was two years and six months old when she cold trailed a hog for over an hour and had gone way over a mile late one afternoon. A top hand said, "Mr. Perry, if she bays that hog, I'll be impressed."

I said, "Really? Get ready to be impressed." She finally bayed, and I humbly said, "Thank you, LORD."

HIGH RIDER

It's not any great wonder that an old-time cowboy don't fit into this modern-day society, especially when he spends time alone and ain't really no people person.

In late December of 1992, I made it back to Texas. After having been gone from this country for several years, a lot of things had changed about my old home range. And it seemed to me there were a lot of strange things happening in the land. More property had been sold and had exchanged hands. Several of the old places now had new fences around them with one big, locked front gate. Every one of these new landowners had several posted signs, but not one "Welcome Hog Hunter" sign did I see.

I was now divorced and back on my own, mostly hog hunting, but as opportunity presented itself, I drew cowboy wages day working whenever I could. When my truck motor blew up, I was without communication, teller system, and no transportation. I didn't have the money to get the truck fixed. I up and sold it rather than tried to explain myself to the social services bunch that I paid child support to. I took to hoofing it (front track, walking), and after a few weeks without transportation, I was offered the use of a good touring car. Now, as bad as I hated to walk, time had a way of changing my attitude about both the car and the green-broke paint filly I was now having to ride.

In the nineties there weren't so many hogs, and I hunted in five different surrounding counties. I drove this car to wherever I was going to hunt and then walked all day. When I was hunting around home, I was riding a paint filly named Easter. I hunted three years when God brought me to the end of myself. I had three good dogs, and one of these dogs (Ol' Bunt) went on to become the second extremely good top dog that I ever owned. In so many ways I was still spiritually blind, for I couldn't see why the extremely good top dogs were so hard to come by. God revealed 1 Corinthians 10:31 (KJV) to me: "Whether therefore ye eat, or drink, or whatsoever ye do, do all to the glory of God." The eyes of my understanding were beginning to be open now as I realized God had laid this dog (Ol' Bunt) into my hand so that I might give God all the glory.

There's a couple of notches difference between just a good dog and an extremely good top dog. The extremely good top dogs I've owned have all been one-man dogs. It doesn't necessarily mean that all one-man dogs are extremely good top dogs; it just happened that the ones I have were. One-man dogs have only one master; they try to please and give their all. One-man dogs are usually a little wild and crazy and will often bite a stranger. They can be brought into subjection by another master, but they are different than all the other dogs.

It's the code of the West that you respect the rights of others and that your rights end when they infringe upon the rights of another. For a lot of years I had gone into some of these old places that were now posted. I was now tying up my horse and walking into these places to gather my dogs. It struck me that I ought to do right and ask permission. I argued with myself about doing this, for I knew these new landowners were unfriendly, un-neighborly, and hard to talk to; however, there was a certain place that a lot of these old hogs went to when you got after them. I decided to visit this Johnnie-Come-Lately landowner by phone first. I introduced myself and told them I hunted hogs and that from time to time my old dogs had run a hog onto this property. I asked if I could have permission to walk onto this property and gather my dogs.

This dude asked me, "Mr. Perry, do you trespass on other people's property?"

I said, "You might call it that. I'm asking permission."

"Mr. Perry, do you know what posted means?"

"Yes, but I'm afraid my old dogs don't."

"Don't hunt hogs nowhere near here, and we won't have a problem."

Now, I was kicking myself for having asked, knowing I'd be turned down for trying to do right. I didn't like his cool, charismatic way. It struck me there was another side of me he hadn't seen; I ought to have tipped him my hat and bid 'em good day. Instead, I said, "Neighbor, we don't have any problems, for I was here first."

He went from being cool to real hot. I must have stirred up his Indian. He snapped, "What's that supposed to mean?"

"You, being new and un-neighborly, probably don't know that in the old West it's called squatter's rights."

"Never heard of it. But I'm going to tell you now that if our riders catch you or your dogs trespassing, you will pay the maximum penalty by law. We will prosecute you and the dogs. Is that understood?"

I suppose a smile might be considered as an answer, for I never said nothing, just hung up the phone. What a lot of folks don't know is that if you spend a lot of time with your stock, it's apt to take on your personality. Example: a rough hand is likely to have rough dogs and a snorty, bucky kind of old horse. I happen to be a little crazy, but I like my horses gentle and trustworthy; that could be why I like a one-man dog.

I had stayed away from that part of the country for several months, not wanting any trouble with anyone. But accidently, and not on purpose, it happened that I'd gotten after a long distance running a hog that went straight to this place that me and my dogs were not welcomed at. I followed in behind my dogs on foot. When I got there I knew better than to go into this place. Sometimes you can know better but not do better. I went ahead and followed my dogs.

The roads had been traveled a lot and were beat out. But I was fighting brush, not traveling down a road. My old dogs weren't in there very deep, but I had to get fairly close to stop them. It came to me that they (landowner/riders) would be there waiting for me to gather my dogs and that was how they intended upon catching me. I thought to myself, *That's all speculation unless you go down there and have a look-see!*

I was on top of a little hill, the dogs about six to seven hundred yards below me, most likely in the branch that had water in it. I decided I'd stay put until dark before I started calling my old dogs. The bad part was, unless there was some moonlight, I was probably going to have to stay the night somewhere there myself. Just thinking about it made me thirsty and hungry.

About dark I heard someone whistle, and then they went to calling, trying to catch my old dogs. That spooked my old dogs, and I heard one dog go to booger barking at someone. Now, I've got a warped sense of humor, and I just up and blew with my old goat horn (what I call my dogs with) like it was a bugle, just like a Calvary charge. It struck me again that what's funny ain't smart! Those riders would have me cut off now from the nearest way out of there to where I'd park the car. Therefore, I went the long way in the dark. All my old dogs were there at the car waiting on me and booger barked at me until I spoke to them. I was thankful none of them had been caught, but being in the wrong doesn't make it right.

I stayed away from that part of the country until one day these folks sold out. From time to time me and my old dogs still go there. Just as if I had good sense.

While I was talking to one of these new landowners, he said,

"Mr. Perry, I hear you hog hunt, that you're apt to follow your dogs onto posted property."

I smiled, for he had me pegged out, and I said, "Yes, sir. How about you give me a key to the front gate?"

"I won't give you a key to my lock, but you can put your lock into my lock, for you're welcome to kill all these hogs that are on my place."

THE FAMILY BIBLE

On August 19, 1925, according to Mother and Dad's old family Bible, they had gotten married. Neither of my parents came with much of a dowry. Mother came with a frying pan, a couple of pots, and two big, heavy quilts. Dad had a young Jersey milk cow, a saddle horse, and a pair of dogs. Dad told me he had saved a little money, but it didn't appear to me they had much to set up housekeeping.

Dad was a farmer from his heart and had leased the old Kellum Springs place (an old historical health resort) west of Singleton, Texas. The large main house had a long front gallery (porch) on the south side, with a dog run through the middle that separated the house into two rooms, a cook shed to the north, and two large rooms with a tall fireplace on both the east and the west sides with single bedrooms. A hall connected the long dog run toward the north and connected onto the cook shed. There was a large bathing pool that was made for the sulfur spring water that Dr. Kellum used with his treatments. All of this was built back in the 1800s before the Civil War. The old Springfield road ran from Springfield, Missouri, to Anderson, Texas, passing through my present-day property only a short distance from the main Kellum Springs house. There were several tenement houses, a crib, and stables. A lot of these old structures remain even unto this present day.

Dad had chosen this place mainly because of two creeks that ran fairly close together for over a quarter mile before they forked. All this land was overflow country in big rains. This left silt to settle on top of the ground, making the bottom land rich and fertile. Back then there weren't any kind of commercial fertilizers. The old-timers called this type of soil "made land."

Being a young cowboy, I had cocked my head when Dad said a married man didn't need a horse and saddle. He lightly smiled and said he'd swapped the horse and saddle in on a pair of poor, young, small mules and had to give fifty dollars to boot. There was a severely bad drought in the year of 1925. Not only was water scarce, but folks were chopping down moss trees in the bottoms to moss-feed cattle. Dad said that it was so dry you could hardly get a plow in the ground in most places but that he'd managed to get this made land flat-broke with a small, eight-inch turning plow. He had then gotten a drag and logged this broke ground down.

With a lister (plow) he was able to get all the land bedded (rowed up). Although his mules were poor and green (unbroken) when he'd bought them, they now worked just fine. He had managed the year before to make a good corn crop with his dad. He was able to get a wagonload of corn from home; however, Dad said that all his money was about gone as he tried to make things stretch until he could make his first crop. Most folks don't know that nearly everything will eat corn. They ground corn for cornbread. Mom scalded corn meal for the two dogs. The milk cow ate nubbins (small ears of corn), and the mules ate ear corn also. Dad had to save back a couple hundred pounds of yellow dent corn for seed. My mom and dad weren't complainers; they were just a couple of hard workers.

It was on into the winter when Dad said they had gotten a little rain, but the cold north wind had dried the ground. Dad was able to get his corn planted early in February and had gotten it up to a good stand. He'd plowed it a few times that spring and was ready to lay by (last plowing) in May; however, all corn needs at least one-half inch of rain in June while the corn is tussling and silking in order for it to make. If the corn doesn't get that good rain in June, the corn will burn and will not yield as much per acre. Old-timers called small ears of corn "nubbins."

Dad said the LORD was mighty good to them and they had gotten a good rain that June. That fall he and Mom had pulled and filled their crib full of corn. Dad then did a little trading around and came up with a big, white piggy sow, a couple more milk cows, and another saddle and horse. Mom also had raised a big garden and now had a pantry stocked full of canned goods. Mom had also gotten two laying hens with settings of eggs by that fall. Mom and Dad milked those three cows, and she made butter. She was now able to ride this horse, with two big homemade saddle pockets filled full of eggs and butter, over to the Nidax Sawmill and sell her produce to the sawmill store for strip (sawmill money). In return, she would buy all their staples (coffee, flour, sugar, material, shells, etc.) from the sawmill store with the sawmill money.

Dad once told me that this pair of dogs he owned when he and Mom married proved up to be one of their more valuable assets. Back then nearly everyone in the country had dogs and hunted during hide season (January and February) every night. Dad said that nearly all the folks were in the woods from dark until after midnight.

Now, it was just Dad's way that he could lay back and within five minutes be sound asleep, snoring. He said with so many people in the woods early, he'd sleep until three or four o'clock in the morning then get up and hunt until daylight. A lot of the time he'd ride his horse several miles from home to hunt some other territory. After daylight every morning he'd get a mess of squirrels for their dinner on his way home. After cleaning and stretching all his hides, he'd usually spend the rest of the day in the field.

Now, Dad said that there were more opossums and polecats than any other varmints, and on a good night, he'd get from six to ten head of hides. On an average, opossums and polecat hides would bring about ten cents each. He said that a good, average-sized coon, around a twenty-inch hide, would bring one dollar. A fox or bobcat would bring a couple dollars more. He said that coons were scarce and that he didn't catch but one or two a season. Dad also had a few steel traps that he used when he caught sign of a fox or of a bobcat; these also were scarce, and he would catch only a couple of them during hide season. Dad sold his hides mostly to Montgomery-Ward. He said that you shipped the hides and they would grade them and send you back the money. Any hide caught early (before season) or late (after season) usually wouldn't grade. The hair would slip (come out) off the hide or the hide itself would be a dark blue, and no one would buy those kinds of hides.

Back then Dad was one of the few who had a high school education. He'd been taught by the New England Primer and was good at ciphering (numbers) also. Now, Mother enjoyed hearing Dad read, and being as there weren't many newspapers around in this country, Dad took to reading the family Bible after supper every evening. It wasn't long before some of the neighbors found out Dad read the Bible in the evenings, and they'd walk over to hear the Bible read and then walk back home after dark.

God had blessed the union of Mother and Dad as they began putting some land together. Dad accumulated a lot of hogs after a few years. Pork got high during World War II, and Dad went to gathering and shipping hogs. Their oldest son, R.B., had joined the U.S. Armed Forces, and Mom and Dad had also moved about five miles closer to Singleton on the old Crawford place. This old home, where I was born, still stands today.

Dad had an old battery-operated radio as I grew up. Every morning at five o'clock he'd get the market report with Harry Raisner. Because of their concern for their son and our nation, Dad would get an update on the war. Those were troublesome times, and our nation had turned to God in revival throughout the whole United States. The leaders of our nation were calling upon folks everywhere to lay a hand upon their radio in order to join in prayer as one nation under God, and God moved mightily in the affairs of the people and this nation. The United States of America became a world leader, respected and feared, because we were a Christian nation under God.

My mother and dad were caught up in this revival and had gone to a revival meeting in Roans Prairie, about five miles south of Singleton. There the way of salvation was expounded upon to them (how a person came to understand they were lost in sin, that to be saved you must trust in the completed work of the LORD Jesus Christ for payment for your sin debt). They went forward to make their profession public. It was also at this time that Mother was carrying me.

After they'd settled the matter of salvation, the preacher asked them, "Do y'all want to dedicate this child unto the LORD?"

Mom and Dad had a way of looking at one another and without saying a word, Dad knew if Mother agreed or disagreed. So Dad asked the preacher, "What all does this consist of?"

The preacher told 'em that their part of the deal had to do with teaching and training me up in the nurture and admonition of the LORD, that they were to lead in a family altar of daily devotion and family Bible-reading and take me to church.

Dad said, "We'll do it."

A lot of water has run under the bridge since the time I made it to Texas in 1945. I was raised up going to church, hearing the Bible read daily and hearing Brother J. Harold Smith each night on the battery radio. I always knew that my mother and dad loved me, and I knew I was very special to them. I also knew they were concerned and probably disappointed with me cropping out a cowboy instead of a preacher, for they were expecting a lot more. But all I ever heard them say was, "He's different."

Along about the time I was twelve years old, I'd heard a good bit about hell, and I didn't want to go there. I realize now I've always been plain-spoken, and when I told the preacher, "I don't want to go to hell," I needed someone to expound clearly what it meant to be drawn by God's Spirit and God's Word, what it meant to be lost in sin, what it meant to believe with the heart, to trust the LORD Jesus Christ's completed work upon the cross, what it meant not to be ashamed of the simplicity of understanding these simple truths of God's way, and then to call upon the name of Jesus as Savior and LORD of life.

To have a personal relationship with the LORD Jesus Christ, we supply a sinner; it's God who supplies all the saving. The moment this transformation takes place is called being "born again." Salvation is the beginning of spiritual birth. Lordship of life is when the Spirit has control. Our testimony is our witness. It merely tells of our walk of life and how we came to have a personal relationship with the LORD Jesus Christ. It's simply how we got saved.

When I had a personal encounter with the LORD, I was twenty-eight years old. I'd found that I had been deceived in believing I could have God's will my way. We are saved on God's terms, exactly God's way that's taught in the Bible. We are to examine our own self, to see if we are in the faith. It glorifies God, and our eternity depends on what we do with Jesus.

After an encounter in salvation, the transformation in me brought about a hunger in me for God's Word and a family altar in my own home.

FISHING FOR HOGS 1

*I*t's kind of strange that at the time I was doing the things that I'm writing down I never considered them as worth telling. I never did anything heroic, really nothing out of the ordinary standard of everyday cowboying. All in all, looking back, it's been quite a life, and I guess a cowboy's life is never ordinary. Here's the way a couple of different little deals stacked up that struck me as being a little different from just the everyday run-of-the-mill kind of work that I do.

The setting of this yarn got its start back in the 1960s, when a lot of city slickers started coming back to this country and getting a deer lease. This country around where I live had lots of deer, and deer hunting became popular. It was common knowledge that a deer lease from most landowners, at that time, was the going price of one hundred dollars per gun. If the place had a few hogs to go along with the deer, it brought more, up to as high as two hundred dollars per gun. As the landowner was greasing his pocketbook, he never complained about the hogs; however, there weren't many places that had feral hogs on them.

It was during the 1970s that we didn't make a mash crop (acorns).

All wildlife was suffering for something to eat. A dairy farmer by the name of Mr. Floyd, over to the south of me, was feeding some dry dairy cows and replacement heifers not far from the head of Sand Creek. The dairy farmer's son, Mr. Ronnie Floyd, had seen a hog run off from around this feeding ground and managed to kill a sure-enough big hog. It was some time later when I got word that hogs had been seen on Mr. Floyd's place, so I went to have a look-see. When I rode up to this feed ground about ten thirty in the morning, the cattle had grazed off. Nothing had been there fresh, so I knew that if there were any hogs coming, it would have been probably after dark. However, through all the stomping around of the cattle, Ol' Mitzie and Ol' Junior acted as if they could still smell a hog, though they weren't able to carry the hog's trail.

I circled back around to the north when these dogs picked up on this hog sign. It wasn't long before my dogs bayed, but they didn't sound right. It sounded like they were barking in a hole at an armadillo. When I got there they were in the head of this branch. It was a dry waterfall, and both dogs were barking at the opening down in the bottom of this branch. It was dark back in there, and I didn't see nothing from the back of my horse. Now, I might have been born in the night, but not last night. It could have been a big hog or a little one in there. So I thought I'd try to fish 'em out, and maybe I could talk Ol' Junior into being my bait.

I caught my old trusty gyp, Ol' Mitzie, and tied her with a pigging string to a small tree out of the way. Now, Mitzie didn't like it, but that's how it goes. I took my rope off my saddle and tied the knot end into Ol' Junior's collar, and we eased back down into the bottom of this narrow, steep branch that ran into Sand Creek. If this happened to be a big hog, I realized I wasn't much smarter than Ol' Junior, for I didn't have any place to go but straight up that bank.

Ol' Junior was barking at the opening, but when I said, "Catch 'em," he shot into that cave six or eight feet deep. He'd hushed, and I could hear a lot of commotion, so I went to drawing in my line with Ol' Junior and a sixty-pound shoat out of that hole. He had that hog by the ear. I got the hog by the hind leg and pulled him back about twenty feet. We were far enough that Ol' Junior couldn't go back into this hole until I got this one tied down. We fished out three head of those sixty-pound shoats. I was thankful that there wasn't an old sow or a big hog in there, for there's no telling how this story would have ended if there had been.

FISHING FOR HOGS 2

Along in the 1980s I was living in northeastern Oklahoma, but the strong ties that I had with my mother and dad would often call me back home to Texas. I often would try justifying my trip by bringing a trade horse or two with me. Often I'd hunt a day or two, filling my coolers with hog meat. I'd make a couple of sale barns and buy a dozen or so rannies (small calves). After I got my horses traded out, restocked my cooler with hog meat, and bought a few cattle, I'd head back to the north country.

I had about the same pattern for several years, and everything seemed to be working. I was still paying all the bills and had managed to keep the wolf away from our door. I had kept only the best two dogs of the four dogs that I had in my pack. On the old Box-P ranney operation, in Talihina, Oklahoma, I didn't have anything for a dog to do. I didn't realize that if a dog lay up on a chain, after a while, he would lose a lot of these effective skills, and his capability would be greatly diminished. Hunting once every two months, my two dogs got fat and sorry. I didn't realize what a couple of years of not hunting could do to a finished dog that wasn't hunted regularly.

I was down in Texas and was hunting with an ol' horse trader,

Mr. Grady Stephens, on Kick-a-poo Creek one cold, wet winter day. The creek was almost full. We found hogs that morning and had both killed one each. The dogs had left running a hog down the creek. Now, Grady, who had been a cigarette smoker, had an operation on his throat and had to have a little microphone to talk with called a trake. He walked back and brought the truck as I drug the hogs to an old oilfield road. After I'd gutted and loaded them into the back of his truck, I told him I was going to take in behind my dogs.

He said he would go around to the other side of the creek on another road in the truck and listen. If I heard him blow his truck horn three times, he would have found the dogs. He'd listen for me to blow my horn back. If I found the dogs, I would blow three times (that meant to come quick, I've got a big hog caught). He'd come as close as he could and blow his truck horn to answer and let me know where he was at.

Now, I'd gone down the creek a little over a mile when I heard my dogs baying, but I couldn't hear 'em that good. I'd come upon a log (not very big around) green tree that had fallen across the creek. It was cold, but finally I made up my mind to go ahead and cross this creek, thinking the dogs would probably be more to the southeast. I had my hands full getting across. I had my gun on a sling and swung around on my back, a couple of pigging strings and a dog leash tied around my neck and shoulder, and a lad rope in my hand.

The creek was so crooked that I could not tell what side of the creek the dogs were really on. When I finally came upon my dogs, they were both in the creek and next to the bank. The water was pretty swift, and the hog and dogs had made it to a bend and were barely able to stand along this steep bank. I wasn't much over a foot above this hog when I eased up there and looked over the bank and saw him. I snaked out a loop and dropped it down over this hog's head. Just as he tried leaving, I caught him around the head and one front leg. I pulled him back to the bank and worked my way down to a place where I could reach my dogs. I made 'em come to me as

I pulled 'em upon the bank and out of the creek. Then I put them on my dog lead.

I was busy and had never blown my horn when I looked up and saw Grady coming along not far from me in his old truck on what had to be another oilfield road. He stopped when he saw me there and finally came over to where I was. I had my hog pulled in tight, and my foot was laid upon the rope.

Grady couldn't see the hog as he walked up to me. He just asked, "What are you doing?"

"Fishing."

"You done any good?"

"I got one."

He looked over that bank as the hog *whooshed* at him. He said, "You sure do! Now how are you going to get him out?"

I said, "I caught 'em, and you ought to tie 'em!"

But Grady didn't think so. So I pulled this hog down the creek until I got him to a tree, ran my rope up over a forked limb, pulled him out, and tied him. It really wasn't much to it.

HIGH-BROWED GAL

Having been born a cowboy, I grew up knowing the cowboy way. I've always tried to show everyone proper respect, but more especially to the ladies, by saying, "Ma'am." I never knew what to say to the girls my own age, especially to one of the fair opposite sex that I thought was real pretty. To me, "pretty" is from within and not necessarily an outward appearance. Being nervous, this caused me to appear to be more country, backwards, and shy. So whenever I'd speak to a pretty gal, instead of saying, "Hi!" I got into the habit of saying, "Hey!"

I struggled with school but made it through the eighth grade. That year my sister, Cecile, was a senior. Now, she was having all kinds of school activities. We lived at Anderson, so Mom would wait after Dad got in from Singleton, sometimes nearly dark. Mom would then have to go to Navasota after dark to pick her up. I rode the school bus and then hitchhiked four miles on home. Mom thought we needed another truck. Dad wanted to buy a cheap, secondhand old clunker, but Mom wouldn't have none of that for her daughter. So Dad bought a new 1959 Ford truck, and we drove back and forth to school her senior year.

With all my sister's activities after school, I'd gotten acquainted with several of the high school students. About the prettiest girl I'd ever seen was the sister to my sister's best friend. I always thought that this high-browed gal was a looker, but nobody ever knew it but me.

I had kept this a secret for forty years. One day while I was buying my ol' Dodge truck a tank of diesel, this lady pulled up to the pump on the other side of me. Although I hadn't seen this lady for thirty years, I didn't need to see this lady's name on some running for office card. Now, I knew at a glance who she was. She hadn't changed any. She was still as pretty a lady as she was years ago.

In my own backward kind of shy way, I finally said, "Ma'am, were you Miss Betty…" and I used her maiden name.

She smiled and said, "Yes."

I said, "Ma'am, you probably would not remember me, but I'm Lloyd Perry."

Miss Betty seemed excited and somewhat elated at our meeting. Then, like the high-browed lady she always has been, she seemed astonished that I remembered who she was.

I said, "Ma'am, why would you ever believe that I'd forget who you are? You still look the same."

I never used the word "Hey!" because of another girl making a monkey out of me. I don't think no one knows my secret or how hard a cowboy can fall when he has cocked his hat.

MIDNIGHT OIL

It's been said, "He'll work; he just ain't bad about it." Now, I can only smile, for that's getting down to where I live. I've never had an eight-to-five job or taken anybody's salary in all of these years. I could have, I suppose, for I've had a few job offers. Instead, I chose to go on my own hook, by using the bank and some investments to make an honest dollar.

It's been a good life here in the Old West, especially when you get your priorities in their right perspective and the spiritual life is in line with God's will. Matthew 6:33 (KJV) says, "But seek ye first the kingdom of God, and his righteousness; and all these things shall be added unto you."

In February of 2008 I opened the Singleton wild hog-buying station under Mr. and Mrs. Tarver for Southern Game. At first I was kept pretty busy. I got acquainted with a lot of trappers and cowboy hog hunters from fifty miles around. As the acorns began to fall and the hogs had plenty to eat, the hogs weren't taking traps. Since it was the dead of winter, there weren't any day jobs working cattle. Several of these cow hands turned to hunting hogs to try and make it until spring work got here.

When that Texas hot, dry summer got here in July and August, trappers and hunters were losing hogs from exertion and the heat; however, in the game of life, you've got to take care of business by going early or else taking time to cool out your hogs after you've caught them.

Business fell off, and I went back to riding horses and training dogs. I had sold two young dogs since the first of that year and was now hunting another set of young dogs. These young dogs could be a handful. In order to break 'em off of everything but a hog, it takes practice, practice, practice. When I am able to get my young dogs tired, they begin to know that it's only hogs I'm after. When you push the envelope to the limit, it's not only the dogs that are run down. I'm barely able to get one foot in front of the other. You'll know it if you've ever spent the midnight oil.

LONE WOLF

$\mathscr{I}$had nearly finished my tenure in the north country. My intentions had been good, but my life didn't go like I thought it should.

It was a late autumn evening on the old Box-P rannie operation in Talihina, Oklahoma. The foliage had turned its many different hues of green. It was getting cool and still that evening. I'd finished my choring and was headed toward a large, empty house, when a coyote cut loose with a long, sharp howl. He was soon answered by another coyote a long distance away. Then coyotes joined in from far and wide. These howlings, hackings, and yelpings lasted only a few minutes; and like they started, these howlings stopped abruptly. When an unusual strong and intimidating howl took over and left an eerie chill up and down my back, I knew that was a lone wolf.

I don't recall ever hearing a wolf howl before. I'da known it if I had. It will leave a memory in your mind all its own. Now, only fifteen years later I was experiencing a hot drought of a Texas summer. I'd been getting up at 5:00 a.m. and hunting until 9:00 a.m. But with five young dogs in my pack and a full moon, I was putting two or three hours hunting on them at night. Hunting twice a day after a while began to show and tell on the dogs and me. I knew it would only be but a couple more of these good nights, and then maybe I'd get a little rest. When all alone one evening, I heard a distinct howl that raised the hackles up along my neck and back. I heard that and knew that howl, for I'd heard it before. This ol' wolf was doing a decent encore, without any interruptions. There is a difference that you'll know and feel when you hear the howl of a lone wolf.

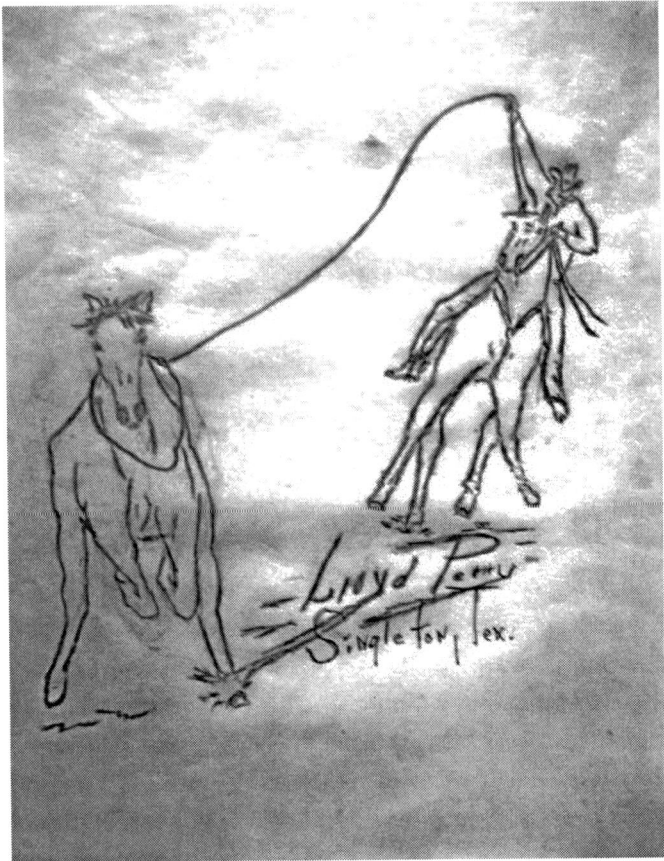

RESCUE OL' YELLOW

As I grew up, Dad had a schoosh (many) of hogs on feed in a two-acre feed lot with a spring branch running through the middle of it at the old Crawford place in Singleton where we lived. Five miles to the west of where we lived, Dad had a twenty-five-acre hog pasture at the old home place called "The Old Place." Dad was running three to five boar hogs on one hundred head of sows.

I can still remember Dad saying to me, "I have lost a little money a few times with hogs, but they paid for the most part of all the land that I've bought." Therefore, every weekday morning, Dad would pull his chair up close to the battery radio and listen to Harry Raisner give the market report at 5:00 a.m., five days a week.

We all ate breakfast a little after 5:00 a.m., for there was some early choring to be done each morning. Dad kept from three to five part-Jersey milk cows. Some were wet (milking), and others were dry. We milked from one cow and had some rannies (nursing calves) on the other cows. The horses also came into the lot and were fed at daylight each morning. Dad would check the feeder hogs. Then we'd go to the old place and feed hogs first thing. This went on seven days a week, 365 days a year. On Sundays Dad would come back home, and we went to church.

From time to time, Dad would notice that his boar hogs had been fighting. He'd say to me, "Catch both of our horses; we've got to go catch that cold-blooded boar hog first thing." The pigs out of a cold-blooded hog would lose money when sold as a top hog.

Although I wasn't very old, it seemed to me that Dad's ol' dogs knew what we were fixing to do. Dad would usually point out to me where the hogs had been fighting. Dad's ol' dogs would begin trailing right there as I'd stay in sight of the dogs. Dad would go to the fence and start looking for that boar hog's hole where he'd come in. If the hog wasn't in the hog pasture and those dogs happened to lose his trail, the boar hog would usually come in and go back out the same hole. If Dad got to this hole first, he'd be waiting. If the dogs and me got there first, I'd lope up and go find Dad.

Most of the time the hole would be on the south or west fence line. The south fence was next to Dad's bottom cornfield, which was also hog-fenced with net wire. If the hog went west, that usually meant that the hog was coming up Gum Creek from Gibbons Creek. There were several switch cane thickets that hogs liked to lay in. If the hog went south, he'd be in thick, piney woods and yaupon thickets. We'd go out of one of three gates and ride back to the hole in the fence. Dad would start tracking to get a course on which way the dogs went, for you can't track a hog or a dog very good on pine straw. As we'd ride pretty well straight with the way, Dad had coursed (that the hog had left); it was my job to listen for the dogs, for Dad was hard of hearing.

When I'd hear the dogs baying, I'd tell Dad in what direction I had heard them. When we would get to the dogs, Dad would ease in to see what they had and if it was a good place to catch this hog. If it was a real thick thicket or a berry briar patch, Dad would ride his horse in on that hog and make 'em run out of the thicket. Those two dogs didn't catch a hog; they just bayed until Dad said, "Catch 'em!" The gyp (Lilly Bell) would hit the hog in his back end, usually on the hock. The hog would spin around or sometimes just squat. The red ring neck dog (Old Red) would catch the hog by the jaw, and those two dogs would hold that hog.

Dad would ride up, shake out a small loop, and drop it down about the hog's mouth. When the hog bit his old throw rope, Dad would jerk it tight, up over the hog's top teeth and around his nose. Dad would wrap the rope around his saddle horn and take up the slack. He'd say, "Get out!" one time to those two dogs, and they'd turn that hog loose. Dad would tie the hog up high to a tree. The hog would stay set back upon that rope until he was thrown and tied down by all four legs and loaded, usually up on the back end of Dad's tractor and shredder. Dad would unload him off the shredder and cut the boar (making him a barrow) and untie him inside his old stable that was walled up, bull tough, stud-horse high, and pig-tight. This same old routine went on until up in the 1960s, when Dad sold out of the hog business completely.

I graduated from high school in 1963. There was only one fellow in our country that still had good-blooded hogs, Mr. Charlie McGregor. From time to time I'd cut sign of a cold-blooded boar hog that was going to his hogs. I'd take to 'em, catch 'em, cut 'em, then eat 'em just like I'd been taught and was raised up doing, except I wasn't as good of a man or the dog trainer that my dad was. He's the only man I ever saw who could catch a hog and never get off of his horse.

In the summer of 1981, Mr. Charlie had a single wild boar hog coming to his hogs and whipping his boar hog. Now, ol' Charlie never called me by my given name. I was and always have been "Cowboy" to him, and he asked me to take to that wild boar for him. I'd tried this old hog two or three times and had missed him. Finding only old signs that were a day or two old, my dogs would try to carry it but kept coming back, restarting at the same place. After trying this hog a few times, I finally got into sign that was made early that night before, and the dogs and me got there about 10:00 a.m. The dogs carried this hog back to the south. By the time they worked 'em over to the piney woods, about a mile and half away, the sun was hot, and the dogs didn't take it very far into the piney woods on that pine straw until they'd start returning to where they'd already been and try to restart the sign again.

Nearly a week later, it had finally come a good shower. The hog had walked after the rain that night. When I got there on horseback about 7:00 a.m. or 7:30 a.m., those three dogs took to that sign and got away from me on this not-so-good, green-broke, stubborn Oklahoma four-year-old horse that I called Red Man.

Now, I was still living in Texas. I was about thirty years old and was riding out a couple of young horses and selling them each year in the spring. I had bought two Okie four-year-old horses that I thought were cheap. I'd been buying my horses in Texas, and what I'd saved in a few dollars in buying these two Okie horses wasn't nowhere near worth the trouble and the extra headaches I encountered for the next nine months. Both horses were four years old, green-broke, and spoiled.

That spring, Mr. Bill Bay had a ten-year-old, good-looking, bald-faced stocking-legged horse that had too much white up on his legs to get quarter horse registration papers. The horse had a little gimp in his step but wasn't crippled. His real problem was that if you ever roped anything on him, you'd best not try and pull it by the saddle horn, for he'd spin around and wrap you in the rope. This is called "cutting you down." One of my Okie horses would kick; we had us a trade, but neither one of us did the other no favor in the trade. We just changed age and color and a different bad habit.

I was sitting at the Madisonville Sale Barn waiting on a little hamburger and wondering whatever happened for them to have made such a sorry grade of coffee so weak you could read a paper through it, when an old-time horse trader, Mr. Grady Stephens, came into the café and pulled up a chair, saying, "You look like you lost your last friend."

I responded to that by saying, "It wouldn't have been no trader if I did, for a trader don't have a friend."

He laughed and said, "Something's bothering you. What is it?"

"It's disgusting anymore: from this cheap, watered-down coffee they sell to not being able to have a decent trade and having a long-distance boar hog that's been putting it on me, even down to the company a man has to keep that wants to know all his personal business."

"Everything's going to be all right, kitten."

I sat up straight and said, "What's this 'kitten' business? You've always been crazy. You ain't gone strange too, have you?"

"Naw! You know me better. But you can cry your little heart out to old Grady."

About that time a waitress came over to my table to take his order. He told her, "Make a fresh pot of coffee and put some coffee in it; then bring us both a cup. This friend has a real problem, and I'm going to try to help him solve it." He went on to say to me, "Don't do nothing crazy like shoot yourself. Old Grady will be at your house in the morning at four, and he'll help you work this problem out."

This waitress was looking at me as she hurried away. In a little while she was back with two cups of real black java, blacker than three feet up a stovepipe. She took Grady's money, but she kept watching me out of the corner of her eye. Now, I don't mind folks thinking I'm from way out west, but I didn't like the thought of someone thinking I was mentally touched or crazy enough to shoot myself!

The next morning Grady got to my house at 4:00 a.m. just like he said. I had Ol' Red Man saddled and was working on a second cup of java that would have easily floated a horseshoe. I'd been leaving horseback and riding four miles then starting to look for the sign of this hog. Instead of the usual, I was going to throw in with Grady. I put my dogs and my old stainless steel thermos bottle of coffee in Grady's truck.

Now, Ol' Red Man wasn't used to no ride in some old rickety trailer, and he would not go into it. I backed Grady's horse out, and Ol' Red Man still wouldn't go in but tried pulling away from me. I didn't like what was happening, so I took off my bridle to keep 'em from breaking my reins. I then made me a war bridle to tie the other end of my rope inside of that trailer. I took another rope and put it over his rump. I led him up to that trailer, and he stopped. I pulled my war bridle, and then I nudged my rump rope as he began backing up. When it didn't check him, this war bridle began to tighten; when I jerked down hard on the rump rope, he jumped forward but to the side of the trailer. Then he went flying backwards, trying to pull away, but that war loop bridle sucked up around his neck and jaw, causing him to rear up and try jumping over Grady's trailer.

When he landed, he hit flat on his side, busting one of my stirrups. He got up shaking. Now, I was plenty mad but somehow kept control as I looked at my stirrup all mashed up. I said to Grady, "I got another horse, and I believe I'll saddle and ride him."

Grady said, "Good idea."

Having chunked another piece of leather on the sorrel Bill Bay horse, I slapped a halter on old Red Man and tied 'em up high to a gentle tree limb where the brown horse had dug out a two-foot hole. I loaded Ol' Wild Bill, and we took off hog hunting a little before 6:00 a.m. We lost about an hour's time and a busted stirrup; it would have saved me time and money just to have rode Ol' Red Man.

We got back in around 2:30 p.m., for we never found a hog track and had never cut any sign. I told Grady that being as he was old and his horse was soft, I'd let 'em off early and we'd go in early. What was really bothering me was that bay horse and my busted-up stirrup. As soon as I unloaded Ol' Wild Bill, I told Grady to wait a minute. I went and got Ol' Red Man, and he loaded and unloaded two or three times, just like a dog. I told Grady, "You must have hauled a goat, for your old trailer stinks!"

"Naw! That ignorant horse had rather walk than ride, and if you're taking up for him, then you've both got a mental problem."

"It wouldn't hurt for a stinking old horse trader to wash up his trailer and bathe himself every now and then so that he and his old trailer don't smell like a goat."

"I'll be here early tomorrow, so load your horse this evening, and we'll go in your rig tomorrow."

"Go on home and get washed up, and there won't be a problem with me or my horse riding with you."

True to his word, Grady was at my house early the next morning. Ol' Red Man hopped up in his trailer like a dog. We made another round but never cut any sign again. Next morning we did the same thing, only this time the hog had been there earlier that night before. The hog had come from the west and went back the same way toward Gibbons Creek. Tracking systems weren't heard of. I used a turkey bell tied to a dog's collar. When the dogs hit that cold sign, they pulled out of sight but not out of hearing distance of that bell, as they still were working the hog sign. I had to ride up in order to get to a gap and then get back in hearing of that bell. Having missed Grady and his dog Ol' Yellow, they finally came on. Ol' Yellow, Grady's faithful, trusty old dog, didn't make the trip with my dogs. When I asked why and what was wrong with that pot licker, Grady's excuse was that his dog didn't know what my dogs were running.

I asked, "How do you usually communicate with that pot licker?"

He said, "Hold on, and I'll show you."

Now, Ol' Yellow had laid around in Grady's yard all day in Madisonville and acted like he wanted to bite everyone that came along except Sammy Lions and me. Then he prowled all over Madisonville all night. For that reason, Grady had taken to putting Ol' Yellow in the trailer in the evening before we'd go hunting. I went to riding north and then south, listening as I pushed west. Grady thought Ol' Yellow was doing some kind of good work, for they were trailing the dogs and the hog. But after a while Ol' Yellow gave it up. My dogs had gone a long ways with this hog, but we never were able to find them. The dogs all came home later that night.

The next week Grady didn't show up. I'd gone across Highway 30. I rode from Gibbons Creek bottom east up Peach Creek and didn't cut any sign. I made a loop across Gibbons Creek, back to where there was another crossing that had washed out. I finally got across Gibbons Creek and into the old Burger bottom at nearly dark. I had to go the long way with some roads, for that was one of the darkest nights I ever remember. It was so dark I had to just give Ol' Red Man his head and see how bad he wanted to be fed and be shed of that saddle. I could not see my hand stuck out in front of me. If he'd missed a turn, we'd have had to lay out until the next day. But we made it in about nine thirty or ten o'clock that night.

Next morning Grady showed up while I was still waking up a cup of coffee. I had my horse fed, but it wasn't saddled. I said, "I believe that hog goes all the way to the Navasota River, for I cut sign way down Gibbons Creek, some that was old then some that was a lot fresher."

Now, I'd been looking for that hog for over two months and hadn't found him. Hogs move around to wherever there's feed, for I had noticed most of the sign was on Gibbons Creek; however, we hadn't found much sign anywhere else.

It was beginning to turn into the fall of the year. Mornings were a lot cooler, and the trees were beginning to turn their many hues. Sweet gums and black gums were my favorite dark-purple red colors. God had made this a special time, for a cold, rough winter wasn't far away. I kept riding and looking and had about decided that this hog had moved to a completely different range.

I hadn't seen hide nor hair of Grady for nearly three weeks when he called my mother, for I couldn't afford the luxury of a telephone *and* hunt hogs too. He asked if Dad would stop by my house and give me the message that he'd be at my house early the next morning and go hunting and for me to call him back if I couldn't go hunting. The next morning he rolled in at about 5:00 a.m. We sat around and drank up the rest of a gallon of coffee. Deer season was going to be starting within a couple of weeks. The woods were already filling up on weekends with hunters. There was already enough shooting to cause me to think they'd started the shebang early. I'd been riding southwest and west when I said, "Let's ride over to the southeast part of this old range. Looking for that boar hog is about like looking for a needle in a haystack."

Grady said he didn't care where we rode because hunting with me didn't produce any pork no how, but at least he got his horse rode.

I started not to even answer, but I said, "You don't keep a horse but a month or two. I don't know why you even ride 'em." Sure enough, Grady came out with a good-looking little compact mare that he said he might keep for a hog-hunting horse. I too had gotten rid of Ol' Wild Bill, the bald-faced, stocking-legged horse, and was riding a black horse that came from a top hand, Mr. Sam Richards of Broken Bow, Oklahoma. That horse was bred and raised in the Warehouser cuts and was a good woods horse. His head was a lot like mine: long and rough and a might hard to look at. He was big for a four-year-old, and the hair on his fetlocks told me that some of his ancestors had probably pulled a plow. He was gentle and rode good, and I was hoping he'd make a little money for a change, for the last two Okie horses hadn't been nothing but trouble and had lost a little money.

We'd gone over to the southeast part of my old home range. We were riding in a clear cut down an old logging road when we came to a dry wash where these log trucks had knocked out a big hole in the logging road, and the clay bottom of this hole had a little water. There was a fresh hog wallow in that water. My old dogs took to that sign and had a single sow bayed in about fifteen minutes, out in this cutover pine and yaupon thicket. I hurried up and got there, for I'd come by a sure-enough rough dog that had immediately nailed this sow. I got her caught and tied and was having a time getting her drug out of that thick underbrush. I finally managed to get back to this logging road when Grady came up from behind me on this logging road, riding his mare, who decided she didn't like the smell of this hog. I was dragging this hog by its head and mouth when I heard something go *thump* and looked back behind me. The horse Grady was riding was headed the opposite direction, and Grady was lying on his side in this sandy log road.

I said, "Mr. Stephens, are you resting?"

"Yeah. That mare bucked me off."

"Naw! She might have turned out from under you, but you fell off."

"Have it your way. Just go catch her for me."

I asked Grady if he was hurt or had any bones broken. He said he didn't think so. I said, "I'm going to drag my hog back to that wallow. It may take me until tomorrow to catch that mare. But you'll be all right with water and a whole hog to eat."

It didn't take me but thirty minutes to finally catch that horse and get back. Grady had walked down to where the hog was laying in the wallow. He was rocked back on his haunches with his arm around his knees, puffing on a cigarette. There must have not been but this one hog, for the dogs had all come in and were laying under some pines in the sand. I just handed Grady his mare and was telling him to cut a piece of rope so he could tie himself to that saddle, for I was heading to my truck with my hog and was through chasing after his stock. Ol' Yellow was hot and hassling, for the hog was laying in the water hole. He got up from his scratched-out hole in the sand under a small pine tree and was going to check in with his master, Grady. As he walked behind Grady's mare, she laid one on him, kicking Ol' Yellow right behind his right front leg. Ol' Yellow was a pretty big dog, and she almost knocked 'em down. But he ran sideways maybe ten or fifteen feet back and then went to making a small circle going around and around, like he was chasing his tail. After he had made eight or ten of these tight little circles, Ol' Yellow lined out back the way I'd just come from with the horse.

Grady was up on his feet looking down the road, and just like that old Indian who lost his dog, Grady was saying, "Dog gone!"

I said, "Mr. Stephens! Hand me that mare!"

As he handed her to me, I said, "Walk around behind her and get you a dose of that so you can rescue Ol' Yellow. I'm giving out a-chasing your stock."

"Ol' Yellow will be all right when he gets his air, but I'm not riding this mare. I'll lead her or drag the hog on your horse."

"Lead her, for I don't ride other folks' horses, and if I did, she'd kill all my dogs before I could get to the truck. My dogs are going to follow me, and I think more of the least one of those dogs than I do that mare."

Grady said, "Take the hog and the dogs onto the truck. Then come back after while and get us."

I said, "Man! You're a lot of trouble. Give me that mare, and don't you say nothing if I go to hooking 'er."

I stepped into the middle of the mare and rode her up toward that hog. The hog moved, and we were headed the other way faster than I could tell it. I pulled her up, but she didn't want to come back. I over and undered her with some long bridle reins. When she spun one way, I drove my hooks into her shoulder, making her turn back and face that hog. When she tried turning the other way again, I hooked her, and she bit at my boot. I kicked her in the nose and made her stand. When I saw Ol' Yellow standing in the road watching the show, I said to Grady, "Call Ol' Yellow, for I'll see you at the trailer."

PLAY DOMINOES

Around on the inside of my house, I've got a lot of trinkets—not anything that a decent woman would allow to be on display, but several things that would fascinate most any good young cowboy. There's everything from a real big hornet's nest to fifty to sixty big-tooth boar hog skulls, of which some are European, mounted up high in the gable ends of my cathedral-ceiling log house. There are a lot of old Western drawings that I drew, sixty-seven domino trophies, an old-time corn sheller, a few good buckhorns, a couple of mounted bobcats, wood ducks, and two big boar hog heads mounted on the wall. But one of my most prized possessions is an old metal and glass candleholder with a nail ring at the top to attach to the ceiling of a dark room for light. It's old, and I'm simply old-fashioned. I'd thought about using it and cutting off that forty-watt light bulb.

It was in the early spring of 2002, and we were having a big straight domino game at my house. There were five of us playing. When you won a game, we'd mark it down on paper so as to see who was the toughest. If the man sitting in front of you won the game, then you sat out until the next game. This is called "hold-your-man cutthroat straight dominoes."

The man sitting out asked my brother Jim if he'd been fishing lately. Now, this brought on a five-minute fish story and another five minutes of them carrying on like a bunch of old women. So I finally said, "Play dominoes!" However, they weren't through with their chitchatting around. (My daughter Lee makes me put warning labels on any old tale that I make up.)

Finally, after saying, "Play dominoes," the second time and they were still carrying on like a bunch of old women, I said, "Y'all see that old candleholder?"

Mr. Gene Hurt (who was sitting out and was the cause of all this commotion) said, "I've always wanted it. Where did you get it?"

I said, "I don't want to get shed (get rid of) of it, and it ain't for sale. I found it a while back while hunting on TMPA Lake."

Mr. Gary Crawford asked, "Was it washed up on the shore?"

"Not exactly. I just happened to ride up on it. It was bright shining, out in the lake in about knee-deep water."

They were all grinning when the fisherman said, "That's got to be a mighty big lie."

I said, "It's just an old tale that I made up. Now, if you'll knock twenty pounds off that fish, I'll blow out that light." Everyone but the fisherman laughed, so I said a third time, "Let's play dominoes!"

OL' LUTHER
BETTER KNOWN AS: "WILL CATCH A CALF"

There are different ways in which ranches might work their stock in this modern time. Small-time ranches might ride a feed sack and "sook" (called) cattle into a trap and then on into a pen. Large ranches often round up cattle then use a rope hand. From the back of a horse, the rope hand will rope and drag the calf that needs working to a fire. One or two men at the fire will throw the animal on the ground. One man holds on to a front leg of the animal as his knee is planted on top of the animal's neck. While his other knee is in the calf's back, another man grabs the animal's hind leg and holds it straight back and pushes the animal's bottom leg forward with his foot. Another man will do the branding while another uses a knife and often runs the needle (giving shots).

The larger ranchers that are in our country often have more than one pasture, and they're often scattered around. They will pen all the cattle on each place using a hand on a gate horse (type of cutting horse) to separate the cows from the calves. The cows are often worked down a chute and then turned back outside. The calves are often pushed into a smaller pen and worked by hand. It depends on whom you're working for as to how much help they have. Some ranchers hire only two men to pen the cattle and work all the calves, while other ranchers might have four or five riders to pen the same number of cattle and do the same amount of work.

In the 1960s and seventies, I was day-working for twenty-five dollars a day, doing whatever needed done by myself. Common labor was drawing five dollars a day. I soon took the attitude that if it couldn't be done from the back of a horse, it wasn't worth doing. Although my dad never directly said it, I'm sure that he thought I'd crop out a failure for sure. He constantly reminded me there was a lot more to life than staying horseback and riding, which I did 90 percent of the time!

When I got back to Texas from the tenure up in the north country in 1993, cowboy wages were being paid fifty dollars a day. But without the three basic tellers (telephone, telegraph, and tell-a-woman), I had limited communication with the rest of the world. So I mostly hog hunted and trained dogs. I thought I was fortunate to get in on a couple or three days of cow working each month. That would meet my bills.

Then in 1997, day work went up to one hundred dollars a day. Ol' Luther and I had a heck of a good year hunting hogs the year before. The hog market broke (fell) to less than half of what a hog brought in 1996. Luther, my old hog hunting pard, shanghaied me and took to day working. He was in his twenties and probably in his prime; I was in my fifties and on my way out. I did a little day work, but I was afraid one of those younger men might say, "Mr. Perry, I remember when you used to be good help." Now, that wouldn't have set well with me. So I got to looking at my options, and right out of the clear blue I got this idea. But it was going to take some time to get it going again. In years past I'd run a high price shop selling horses and dogs that I'd trained, but that is time consuming.

In the meantime, I did what I had to do to keep the wolf away from my door. I took some of Dad's advice and put in a garden. I cowboyed around the sale barn enough to get a few day jobs and did a little trading on cattle. From time to time I'd see my ol' hunting pard and say, "Let's go catch a hog!"

He'd only smile and say, "Sorry, ol' chap, but my datebook is full for all of next week. I'd like to, but I can't go with you."

Now, my dad and Luther were made a lot alike. They both were built like a stump (from the ground up), not all that tall, just thick and solid; and neither of them knew their strength. In Luther's day he was quite the ground man while working cattle. He could flat walk through a pen of 200-pound to 275-pound Charolais-crossed calves. Whenever someone would pop off and say, "Boy, What's your name?" or "What do the folks call you?" he would say, "They call me 'Will Catch a Calf.'" However, he'll always be a Luther to me, Mr. C. J. Luthie. The one and only.

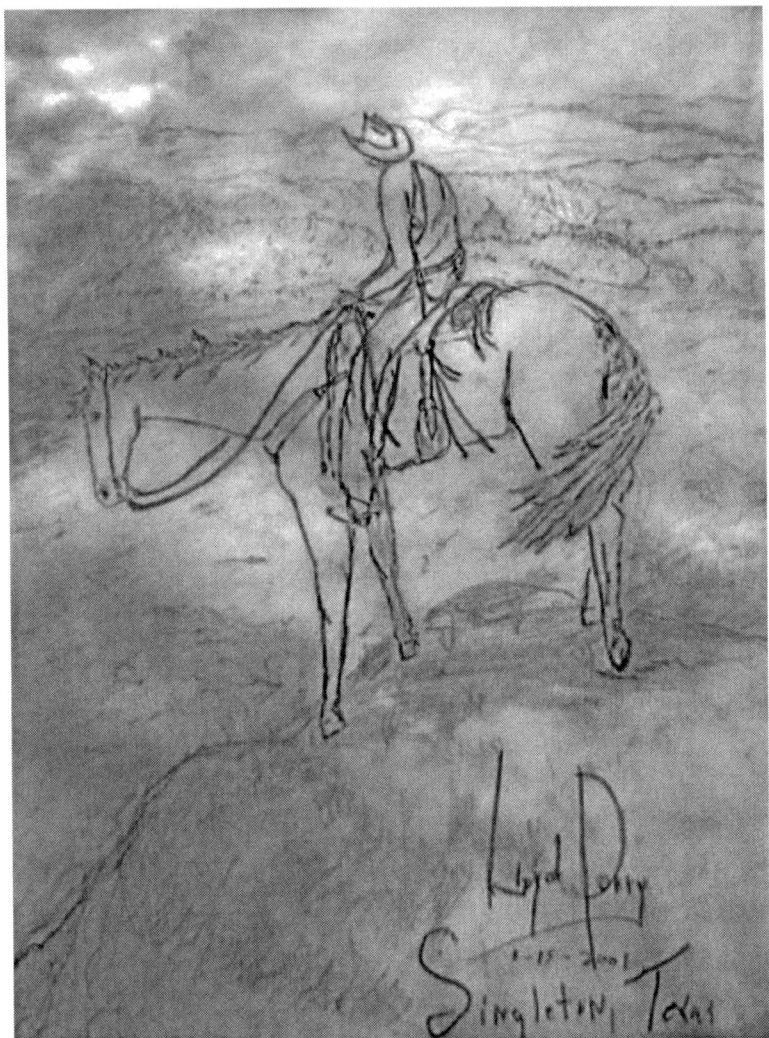

Lloyd Perry
1-15-2001
Singleton, Texas

BILLY CREEK

Back in the late 1970s, after having seen the Osage Country of northeast Oklahoma and northwest Arkansas, it was in my mind to tour around in those ol' mountains of eastern Oklahoma until I could find a ranch that I could buy and fix up or make a land exchange for. Civilization and changes were closing in on me, and that ol' mountain country was still wild and free and years behind the rat race of the modern time. I couldn't do like I wanted to, for I had the responsibility and obligation of a family.

That spring I planned to cowboy around for a couple of weeks riding the grub line and visiting a couple of old friends (stay a week or until I got weak). However, my little venture got turned into a vacation for me, my wife, brother-in-law, and his wife. I took my twelve-foot long gooseneck trailer, with our camping gear in the front and with room to haul a good trade horse back to Texas if I found one handy and worth the money. We spent the first night on the trail at Broken Bow, Oklahoma, with an old friend, Mr. Sam Richards and his family. The next day we pushed on north through the mountains of eastern Oklahoma and came upon a four-mile mountain known as the Kiamichi Mountain at Big Cedar,

Oklahoma. Here I'd gotten acquainted with a Mr. Bill McBride, who told us of Billy Creek State Park. Mr. McBride owned some property up the west prong of Billy Creek that he said he'd like to show me.

Early the next morning, Mr. McBride came to our camp at the Billy Creek State Park to show me that piece of property. When we left camp, we crossed the east and the middle prong of Billy Creek and turned west of nowhere up an old wagon road and went several miles, crossing the same creek twice more. I noticed that when the timber of the national forest stopped, I was looking at roughly twenty or more acres of an old grown-up field. In the mountains, it's rare to find that much good, deep soil in one place. Then I saw an old post and a couple of old, rotten rails. I knew this field had been fenced with rails to keep the stock out a long time ago.

A little farther up this wagon road and to the east side was what remained of an old ranch house made from sawed lumber that was now weathered and had rotted away and had mostly fallen in. From the looks of the trees that had grown up through where this old house stood, I figured I was a hundred years late. The old barn and shed were cratered in also, but I saw several pieces of old work harnesses, tools, and parts of plows and old wagons. Brush had grown up thick where the old crib and stalls had once stood. But there were parts of this old ranch still there. As I kept looking around in the brush, I found two posts side by side. I knew this was part of a big pole corral. This must have been a horse ranch and one of the real deals in its time, most likely an old hoot owl operation (horse thief ranch).

I liked the lay of this ol' ranch; however, Mr. McBride informed me that this was the east half and that he'd bought the west half. That let all the air out of my balloon! We looked at the west half, and it was a nice piece of property but nothing like the east half, with the old headquarter part of this ranch. I didn't say anything about what I'd read into this ol' ranch. I simply was ready to roll up and go north to Siloam Springs, Arkansas, to visit another old-time friend, Mr. Bill Surface, on the Illinois River.

We looked at some high-dollar ranches in northwest Arkansas, and I made one offer to do a land exchange on a place I liked, but things didn't work out. In a few days we turned around in Colorado and drove back to Billy Creek and camped. I bought the west half of this ol' hoot owl ranch from Mr. Bill McBride. There's a little owl found only in that area of those mountains called a horned screamer owl. Believe me, you won't forget that owl if it lights in a tree and lets go of its loud scream when you're in camp. It will flat spook your mule. And if it hadn't have done that *coo-ooh-hoo* at the end, I might have pulled a runaway myself! It's been well a long time since I thought of that little owl, and just thinking about that little scandal booger has gotten me excited and my blood pumping.

About a month after I'd gotten back from our vacation, I went back to the property on Billy Creek. I hired a bulldozer and pushed out a road through the timber, across Billy Creek, and around to the northwest side where there was a high rock ledge that allowed the creek to cut through at its base. I had the dozer to level off a small area on this ledge, and then I built a sixteen by twenty-four log cabin out in the middle of nowhere. My brother Jim, Sammy Richards, and a few other friends all helped me construct this cabin. It took about two months to get it built.

I was going to Billy Creek about once a month, and while cowboying around Talihina, Oklahoma, I kept on looking for an opportunity to buy some ol' ranch. It was in the early spring. I didn't know a thing about calling turkeys; however, I'd gotten acquainted with several folks who did in the north country and had acquired a taste for fried wild turkey breast. I hadn't eaten nothing like it before or after. I'd met an ol' mountain man by the name of Mr. Marion Lou Ellen who was a good hunter and fisherman. An old trader friend (if a trader has a friend), Mr. M.D. Smith of Iola, Texas, had gotten to going up to Billy Creek with me. Mr. Smith was a big feller who could outtalk and outeat anyone I ever met in my life! However, he was able to do most of what he talked about. M.D. was a good-natured feller and liked a good laugh, almost as much as my dad did.

We got to the cabin late one evening, and I said, "M.D., make a pot of coffee while I go up on the side of the mountain and kill us a turkey." Now, I ain't ever hunted or killed a wild turkey in my life and really hadn't expected to see anything; however, I was hoping M.D. would have the truck unloaded and the coffee made by the time I got back. I had barely gotten sat down beside a tree when I heard some noise below me. Now, I knew I'd heard a turkey fly up in a tree. As I sat there real quiet, with my shotgun laid across my legs upon my lap, all of a sudden a big turkey stepped out in front of me so close I didn't have time to get my gun up. I just jerked it up and shot all at the same time. That turkey was so close that I shot this scoundrel booger with the gun almost lying in my lap. I'd seen some shooting like this in the movies, but this was my first time I ever was able to pull off something like that. That shot knocked that turkey over backwards, and he rolled, kicked, and jumped almost to the bottom of the mountain; however, I finally caught up and got my hands on him.

M.D. had the lamp lit and the coffee made when I made it back to the cabin. I opened that front door, and as I threw the turkey through the door into the cabin, I pulled the door shut and hollered, "Clean that one; I'll go get another'n."

It was a mighty cold night that night when I crawled into my sleeping bag on a lightweight aluminum cot. M.D. sat down on the other cot, but it cratered (wouldn't hold up his weight). So he made a pallet upon that rock floor by folding together a blue plastic tarpaulin.

During the middle of the night, something was meddling around on the outside that caused my ol' dog to growl at the front door. Then when he barked, I spoke to him by calling his name. He then lay at the door on the outside of the cabin and growled off and on all night. When that four o'clock alarm clock went off the next morning I hollered at M.D., "Jar the floor!"

M.D. said, "I can't move. I believe I'm frozen solid."

No doubt he had gotten cold sleeping on that pallet on that rock floor. That rock floor was mighty cold on my little feet when I slipped out of that sack and threw some kindling and a chunk of wood into that wood heater. Then I put the coffee pot full of water on the stove to boil and in a hurry got back into my sack.

We went hunting that morning with Mr. Marion Lou Ellen, but we didn't see or kill any turkeys. That evening as my ol' dog growled, I looked up and hollered to the old mountain man, Mr. Lou Ellen, to come on into camp. He had come up the creek, walking and fishing in the creek, and had a string of perch. M.D. and Mr. Lou Ellen cleaned fish while I built a fire for M.D. to cook supper on outside.

Like I said, M.D. was a real talker. But Mr. Lou Ellen was a better listener than most folks, for whenever he spoke he was real low, soft spoken. M.D. had to get up real close in order to hear Mr. Lou Ellen say anything. Now, M.D. was sure that my old dog had been growling at a bear and asked Mr. Lou Ellen if there were any bears in those mountains. I don't know what all Mr. Lou Ellen and M.D. talked about, but on our trip back home, M.D. stated that he'd asked Mr. Lou Ellen if there were any bears around in those mountains.

The old mountain man said, "There are a few, but nothing like they were when I was a kid." He also said that back then there were so many bears that they didn't all have places to hibernate. So bears would break off pine limbs and saplings and pile them up to make a bed to hibernate under until spring.

Mr. Lou Ellen said when he was a boy, the only gun he had was a .22 target. When he'd find a big pile of brush with a bear denned up under it, he'd uncover that bear then stick the .22 target gun inside the sleeping bear's mouth and pull the trigger. The .22 ball didn't kill the bear, but the concussion did.

Now, M.D. had done some hard deciphering. He'd decided that if that .22 ball didn't hit a vital spot, that woken-up bear would make for some bad company. M.D. decided that the concussion probably would have killed the bear. He said, "Yeah! That makes sense!"

I laughed and said, "Anybody messin' around with a bear with a .22 probably ain't all at himself. Sounds like an awful good western to me!"

M.D sat up straight and said, "Concussion would kill a bear."

I only shook my head and asked, "Do you believe that?"

M.D. was in a deep study for a few minutes that seemed like quite a while.

While he was in this deep study, I thought I'd have a little fun at M.D.'s expense, so I said, "M.D., you're a big, talkative Texan. Don't you know when an Okie is putting you up a tree?"

M.D. sat there another minute with his eyes glazed over. He then pointed a finger at me and said, "That feller wasn't lying to me. He don't talk enough to tell a lie!"

THIRTY MINUTES LATE

I was headed down Highway 39 in my truck, pulling three round bales of hay on a flatbed trailer. I was on my way to the Kickapoo pasture to feed some cattle when this dude in an older car blew in behind me and decided to pass me up, all in the same breath. Now, I was doing sixty miles per hour and meeting a truck when this idiot almost got us into a nine-line bind. How we kept from having a collision was a miracle. It's been a while since some idiot has spooked my mule. After it happened and I breathed a sigh of relief and said, "Thank you, LORD!" I thought, *That dude drives like he's from Houston, Texas, or else he's thirty minutes late!* That's what Mr. Bea Mendenhall would have said.

That statement brought a smile to my face, for I hadn't thought of Bea in a long time. Bea was an old time cowboy who had turned horse trader. He liked strong black coffee as well as I do. We'd spent some good times together trading and riding in the mountains of eastern Oklahoma, usually on some fresh new trading stock. We'd take a couple of squirrel dogs and all the makings to fix coffee and dinner. Whenever we'd go someplace together and come across anyone with a loud-sounding car or driving too fast, Bea would always use the statement, "They're thirty minutes late!"

HONEY BEA

When my family and I moved up to the north country of eastern Oklahoma, Jackie Ann was a baby, and she grew up riding all of my old horses. I'd gotten acquainted with an old horse trader known as Mr. Bea Mendenhall. Bea was eighty-nine years old when I first got to know him. Mr. Bea had been an old-time cowboy and thought Jackie Ann was quite the cowgirl of my bunch. Having seen her ride a horse that was way too big for her, he said to me, "That gal needs a pony."

Now, I have always thought an older cow horse was a lot better for a kid horse than a pony. I said to Bea, "That's about as close to a pony that will ever get to stay around here and eat my feed."

A few months later at a horse sale, Bea asked me if it would be all right if he bought Jackie Ann a pony. I shook my head and said, "No, sir, that gal don't need no pony."

Bea said, "Come look at it anyway."

So we went back and had a look-see at this little mare that was a sorrel with a bawled face and one white stocking leg and a flax mane and tail. The pony was only a three-year-old: pretty, young, and lively. I said, "Bea, that horse is about like me; she don't know much and way too much horse for that baby."

Bea said, "Scotty could ride it out of her." I put up an argument about it, but Bea said he'd sure like to buy it for Jackie Ann, so I gave in. Bea bought the pony for Jackie Ann, and she called her new pony Honey Bea, and a handful she was! Scott Perry got about all he wanted and more, for Honey Bea never did ride out gentle. It could be that she had already been tried and spoilt.

ESCAPE GOAT

*T*he year was 1965. I had been day working for a few large ranchers. It was about midsummer when a fellow who had bought some land and cattle on the other side of Carlos, Texas, drove up to Mom and Dad's house. Dad told him to get down and come over and have a chair, for Dad was shaded up under a walnut tree, sitting in a metal lawn chair. There were a couple of extra chairs there. They shook hands, and Dad and this fellow sat down and began to talk.

I was at the barn working on some of my tack. I thought this fellow might be needing some cow work done. I eased up to where they were talking, spoke and shook hands, and then took a chair. I knew that in time if he needed any cowboying he'd bring it up. Instead, it seemed that this fellow had five head of stray goats that were staying with his cattle. He knew that the goats were marked, but he couldn't read a mark. He said that the goats were wild as deer and wondered if Dad had any goats strayed. Dad had him describe the goats as best as a city fellow could, which really wasn't a very good description. Dad didn't think they were his goats. He told this fellow that he didn't know anyone who had any goats missing, but if he heard of someone who did, he'd let him know.

Now, I knew that William Nevells from Cross, Texas, had five head of goats missing, but I kept my mouth shut until after this fellow left. Afterwards I said to Dad, "Reckon five goats would travel twelve to fifteen miles from Cross to Carlos? Back last spring I was working for Mr. Melvin Nevells, and his son, William, had five goats to go missing. I don't know if William ever located his goats or not. That's a long trip for a goat, but the head count is right."

Dad sat there a minute then said, "It's possible. Go call William and see if he found his goats. If you boys go over to this city feller's place tomorrow and take your horses, you all go look first and see if they are William's goats. Then you ask that feller if y'all can take to them horseback. If this feller doesn't care, then you boys be careful that you don't run his stock through a fence." I finally got William on the phone that night, and he said that he had not seen or heard anything of those goats for nearly a year.

The next day when we got over there and I did about like Dad had said, we found that these goats belonged to William, and the fellow said, "Y'all might can pen these goats with my cattle." That had crossed my mind, but without a dog, I didn't think they'd stay with the cattle and told the fellow so.

He said, "Take to 'em and catch 'em if you can."

William and I circled a bad thicket and came through it from the backside upon this opening where these goats were. These goats were out in front of us a little ways in an open pasture with this man's cattle when they saw us and realized we had cut off their escape. They jumped to a full run, and we both took to different goats as they left these cattle. We both caught a goat each, but the other three were long gone. We didn't bother to look for the other three goats. We tied the goats we'd caught and went and got our truck and trailer and loaded them and our horses; as we pulled out, we stopped and told this fellow that we caught two of them.

It was a month or so later, and I was riding fence looking for any place that goats could get out. I rode onto a bunch of Dad's goats lying beside the fence. In just a glimpse, I saw a goat on the outside.

I thought, *That's strange, Dad's goats aren't usually that wild. It might have been those three Nevell goats, but I'm not sure.* I turned my horse around and went and found Dad on the tractor clipping weeds. I told him I thought I'd seen those wild Nevell goats.

The first thing he asked was, "Did you see any of our goats with them?"

I said, "No, sir, I didn't even get to see those goats real good."

The goats that were on the outside were in the Nease land, one hundred sixty acres of solid yaupon and hard wood thicket in the Gum Creek bottom. That thicket was as bad as it gets anywhere around these parts. (It takes two rabbits to get through some of this thicket, one a-pushing and one a-pulling!) It's still just that thick today.

Dad said, "Go back and open our gap going into the Nease land; then get around our goats and push 'em through the gap. Ride east a good long ways, cross the creek, and circle to the south until you come to Joe Shook Jr. branch. Turn back north and go to hollering (like you was driving gentle cattle). I'll go get the truck and walk in with ol' Tommy (his dog) on the east side down to the creek. When you get to the creek, look for sign. I hope there's enough water in Gum Creek to stop our goats from crossing. Mr. Ernest Poteet's fence will hold 'em to the west. Ride to the east side and help me after you cross the creek."

I did about like I was told. When I got back to the creek, it had a good bit of water. I didn't see any tracks on the south side anywhere. I finally got across the creek and heard Dad let loose with a squall

Then he hollered, "Ride east. They got by me."

I doubled back and crossed the creek and circled back to the east. I'd made a big circle and had come to the creek and was now riding west. Dad's old leopard dog named Tommy was with these goats, and I could hear him bark at them every now and then. Goats respected this old dog, for he would catch a goat by the hind leg and then release and then bark. This is what I call "bite." As I got fairly close to the goats and the dog, they moved to the northwest, where

I hoped Dad had held the other goats. I crossed the creek behind the goats but never saw 'em. I took to hollering as I rode northwest. I heard Dad squall a time or two and then said, "Come on. They've all took the gap and are all back in our pasture."

I'd been for leaving things as they were, but Dad said, "No! Get those wild, crazy things penned and back to where they belong. They are subject to leave at any time and take some of our goats with 'em."

I was on a rode-down young horse that on a good day could nowhere near cover a goat like sunshine (be on all sides like he should). But it didn't matter, for we had it to do. We had our trouble at the pen, and I had slipped out a loop.

But Dad was laid-back, talking to me over and over, saying, "Don't use that rope unless you have to."

Strange that Dad repeated his command over and over to me but the dog he only told once. Those goats were all turned facing us, it seemed for a long, long time, when finally one of Dad's old goats took that open gate. Then the tail followed the hide.

This happened several years ago. I don't think I ever told anyone about penning those goats but William. The only thing worth telling was that I got 'em back to their rightful owner.

Strange that in the Old Testament of the Bible it tells of a scapegoat; Jesus became my escape goat when I trusted in the completed work He did for me upon the cross. Now, that is worth telling about. In the day of judgment we all will need a scapegoat.

Lloyd Perry
Singleton, Tx.

RAT READY

$\mathscr{I}$ learned at a tender, early age that you never interfere in other folks' work. When you try to help others do their work, it will soon get to be your work. Housework and milking have always been considered women's work. Therefore, I stayed on horseback! I would be gone fourteen or sixteen hours a day for four or five days a week. Mom, who was a good cook, would have a good square (plate of food) set back on the stove waiting for me when I'd get in. For twenty-six years of my growing up, this was the way I lived life in the Old West.

After I married I didn't see much sense in trying to change or improve upon a good thing. My newlywed wife understood the system, for her dad was an old-time cowboy, who made his living out of a saddle. With beef in the summer and pork in the winter, a little honey, milk, and butter, we lived off the fat of the land for nearly twenty-five years until I was turned out to pasture (divorced). Several different people have helped me build my log home and the setup I have today. Although, I find nothing about housework that I like.

I find myself doing all the work that I failed to see. Not being able to live a carefree life has been hard on me. Cooking is a task that I can't seem to grasp. When I cook a steak, I have to cut it up really small and swallow real fast. It's tough when I ain't got a steak and tough when I cook it. No matter how bad it gets, I ain't rat ready to jump out of the pan into the fire.

TURNIP PATCH

All the years of my growing up, I had to do garden work, but I never really cared for it. I didn't get away from this work even after I was married. So I thought that whenever I moved to the north country I was far enough away from my dad and mom that I could paddle my own canoe. However, that wasn't so, for it was Dad and Mr. Bea Mendenhall that decided I needed a garden and tried turning a pretty good cowboy into a farmer. I never outgrew the influence of my elders, for Bea stepped up and did his best to fulfill my dad's place. Now, I'd never worked in a garden plowing a mule before. Bea was ninety-two years old and a very good teacher. He kept changing tools that I plowed with and would say, "Work in close and you won't have no chopping to do." He didn't know how much that appealed to me.

My hands did not fit a hoe very well; however, Bea would always tell me, "Go slow and take precaution that you don't plow up or cover up the plants."

In time I began to accomplish a knack for handling a mule and a plow at the same time. I began to realize there was a lot of difference in plowing with a mule compared to working the soil with a tiller. It's my own personal opinion; those old-timers knew the best way to work the soil. It seemed to me that the soil seemed more packed when using a tiller or a tractor. I also believe you can raise more produce in a garden with a mule.

This all began in the spring of 1982. Bea was for raising both a spring and a fall garden, and it seemed that I had no option but to do it. We had a couple of good years. In 1984 we had a dry fall in southeastern Oklahoma. I was telling Bea that I was experiencing my first crop failure and that I was going to miss not having a fall turnip patch. I had acquired a taste for eating turnips after having eaten some that Ms. Green had cooked. I was told that she'd boiled them and then fried them down in bacon grease, using a little sugar to take away the bitter turnip taste. After having eaten some of her turnips cooked that way, I decided turnips weren't half bad. The other half was pretty good.

It was a dry fall day that I recalled Bea began telling a yarn. He said back when he was a young man in 1925 that he was farming that year and didn't even get his seed back. That drought was extremely hard on poor country folks and poor cattle. Nobody raised a garden or any other field crops that year. Bea said a little dried-up feller named Scarberry from Talihina, Oklahoma, raised a good turnip patch. Now, ol' Scarberry gave some of his turnips around to the older widow women. It wasn't long after that Scarberry up and married one of these nice-looking widow women. That made me smile, for it looked as if Bea was a little jealous, so I said, "Did you have your hat cocked for this widow?"

"Naw. She'd speak to me and from time to time make a little small talk, but she was never interested in me." I couldn't but help smile as Bea said, "It was a shame, for even one of the widow's children asked their mother why she'd married ol' Scarberry. The widow came back with, 'I can't rightly answer that, but he did have a good turnip patch.'"

I thought that the widow might have hit on something, and I was going to look around and see if there was another Scarberry in that country that might have made a few turnips. Then I'd try and buy a few turnips if possible.

A couple of months later I'd gone off to a couple of fall revival meetings with Mr. Phillip Wade. Now, Phillip was one of the best soul-winning evangelists I ever encountered. Over the course of the years of Phillip's life, he'd gone to several different county jails. After they'd turn those drunken Indians out of jail on Monday mornings, Phillip would often begin to talk to these men as he carried them home. Somewhere within Phillip's conversation he would speak of a personal relationship with Christ. Usually if he won the man, he'd win the man's family to Christ. They would then set up a Bible study and prayer meeting each week, and he'd win someone else in a one-on-one encounter. After a few men and their families were won to Christ, they began to build a church. There were three of these churches within a fifty-mile radius around where we lived.

How inviting this was to me to see how God worked through someone who was willing, yielded, and submitted to the Lordship of Jesus Christ. God can use a man who will depend on him by faith for everything, from the old car that he drove to the gasoline to carry on God's business.

Mr. Phillip Wade was a big Indian who played on the first Talihina state championship football team and knew a lot of people. Phillip liked to eat, and those Indians would feed us both well. I'd just about try anything one time, and these old Indian dishes usually had hominy and hog meat in them. After leaving one of these meetings, I was telling Phillip about the turnips Mrs. Green cooked and about my fall crop failure.

Phillip said, "Check with Mr. McLaughin over on the Fouche Maline. He might have some turnips."

I'd gone over the mountain the very next day and found this Mr. McLaughlin. I told him who I was and where I'd come from and that I had planted some turnips that fall and had a crop failure. Mr. Phillip Wade had told me to check with him, and if he had any turnips, I would like to buy about a fifty-pound sack full.

Mr. McLaughlin asked, "How are Phillip and his mother?"

"They're both doing just fine. Phillip's about God's business, although his health is not very good."

"Come on."

We went by the barn and got a couple of feed sacks.

I smiled and said, "Now, I'm a stranger to you and your country; however, where I come from, when you're willing to buy and you first have to ask the price, it may mean you can't afford it."

Mr. McLaughlin said, "Mr. Perry, I don't have any turnips for sale. I will give you a sack if you will take Mrs. Wade a sack."

I began to notice Mr. McLaughlin's home was upon high ground, not far from the Fouche Maline River. We drove up to his turnip patch, and it was in a small basement, maybe twelve to fifteen feet below this river bottom land. Two small creeks looped around the base of this basement and then went together. There were eight to ten acres of "made land" (silt) in this little basement, and the water table must have been close to the top of the ground. All the rest of the country was brown and burnt up by the heat and the drought. It was unbelievable to see this dark green turnip patch there in this basement, with the roots of those turnips as big as a baseball. When I got out to open the gap that went into this basement, I noticed a couple of red birds as they were singing and whistling upon these tree limbs that leaned out over the bank of the small spring-fed creek below.

I pulled up and was just standing there taking this picture into my memory when Mr. McLaughlin said, "I plant this turnip patch for my cows every year."

"Really? I'm thankful for you sharing your turnips. However, if it is the LORD's will, I'll have turnips come next year."

DAD'S GRANDMOTHER ALLEN

I found this statement to be true: "The tree don't fall far from the stump." It hasn't been so long ago as a young cowboy I'd sit around listening to different old-timers spin some wild tales.

As I grew older, I became aware that my dad had also grown up liking to listen to old-timers talk. One day Dad said that his Grandmother Allen was the best storyteller that he ever heard. Dad was smiling, for no doubt he had seen the strange expression upon my face. Now, a cowboy don't grow up around many women outside of his own mother. I didn't know whether they got together and carried on like old men or not. The only women to ever say anything to me were either reprimanding me for what I'd done or shouldn't have done or didn't do.

Dad began by saying, "All of your aunts, uncles, their children, and any others that were at Grandma Allen's home after Sunday dinner were waiting for church services at Blue Lake that evening and would stop and listen whenever Grandmother Allen would begin to rock in a rocking chair and tell a story."

Grandma Allen came from the Cherokee Nation and was a small woman with a very easy eye and a big smile. Her dining room table was large enough to seat twenty men on heavy wooden benches, with Grandpa Allen's captain's chair at one end of the table. Both of Dad's great-grandparents on the Allen side had died in a cholera epidemic in Oklahoma on their way to Texas. After marrying, Dad's Granddad Allen settled at Piedmont, Texas, and acquired a large land holding. He also built Grandma Allen a large house, which still stands (2009).

Dad said it was the grandkids that would get Grandma Allen to start telling stories about her life in the nations and of the Cherokee people. The children would sit on the ground as his grandmother would usually sit in her rocking chair and tell story after story. Dad said his grandmother was held in such high esteem that even the women and the men quit their visiting and came around and listened also.

Grandma Allen is still highly respected by her people even today. The Allen reunion was started in commemorating her birthday at the Sulphur Springs in Piedmont, Texas, until the early years of 2000.

Lloyd Perry
Singleton, Tex.

A COWBOY TIPS
HIS HAT

*M*r. William Mellman, an old-time cowboy from over at Hempstead, Texas, brought me a pair of puppies in the spring of 2008. I thanked him and told him that I'd take the little gyp (female).

William said, "I brought you the pair."

So I said, "In a case like that, I'll be as nice to you as you are to me and give them back." However, after a lot of conversation, I was to give the dog pup away and keep the gyp.

After a couple of months, parvo killed my little gyp. I'd given the dog to Mr. Bill Bay, an old-time cowboy from Anderson, Texas.

That summer William lost the daddy of these puppies. When I told Bay, he called Mellman and offered him the puppy back.

It was in the late fall, and William and I were working Mr. David Reeves's cattle. William was saying that he didn't understand why that dog puppy wouldn't get solid working cattle. He'd about played out his rope.

I said, "Don't kill 'em. If you want me to, I'll start him for you."

"Uh! You think you can start him?"

"I think I can."

"If you can, I'll take my hat off to you."

"Really?"

After about two weeks of putting up with that dog's ways, I didn't want to admit it, but William might have been right. However, the cowboy humor of seeing him reach and get his hat wouldn't let me quit. Nevertheless, I thought time would change everything, but until then, out of sight and out of mind was the best solution I could come up with. So I put this dog that I was calling Big Boy up at my hog pen that had three head of hogs in it. That way when he barked he'd at least see a hog!

I fed and watered him there at the hog pen, and from time to time I'd send another dog up to the hog pen, and they would bay for a couple of hours. Finally, it dawned on old Big Boy that hogs were his game, and he would bark also until he'd lose his voice.

William came by my house one day, and I said, "Take that old big dog pup when you go. I can't afford to feed a big dog like that." William wanted to see him work but wasn't impressed with a dog barking at a hog inside of a pen.

I said, "You just don't want to reach and get your hat! That's all!"

A month later William stopped at my house, and I got a report that the dog worked but didn't suit him. I said, "That's neither here nor there; you just don't want to pull that hat off!"

"Now, that ain't it. What I got here is a sister to that dog. A dog you'd like—she's crazy. And I can't catch her."

"I ain't got no use for crazy dogs or people if they can't do something."

"She will work both ways and can do something. I just can't catch her."

I named this dog Whirly Bird. Three months later I put on a little dog exhibition for Mr. Mellman in the presence of Mr. Jack Riley. When I said, "Whirly, come here!" she came, and Mr. Mellman's hat was high in the air! Jack was impressed with the four big hogs we caught, but I was more impressed with Mellman's hat in hand.

PERRY LOOK

Very young in life I already knew my vocation and didn't see any sense in pursuing any other professions. Both Mom and Dad were concerned about my carefree cowboy ways. On one such occasion, Dad was giving me an overhaul by saying that I needed to learn to do carpentry work and be able to do some mechanic work. When he finally finished, I said, "Yes, sir, you're absolutely right about one thing. I need to know how to build if I ever have a setup. But I don't want any part of being a grease monkey."

Dad pulled up short and was just staring with his hands folded back on each hip. He made that little hiss sound of air; he pulled through his teeth and did a slight shake of his head, which was his way of letting me know that he wasn't pleased. He was dead serious, and it was to my best interest to keep my mouth shut and let him have it his way.

Finally, he closed the conversation with, "Boy, all I wanted was for you to have it better than me."

DAD'S OLD CEDAR BREAK

*I*n the early years of my life, everyone worked from sun-up to sundown. Family members took care of family, and folks had time to help each other. Anyone that was fortunate enough to land a paying job took care of business. Very few had money to pay anyone wages. There were a lot of folks unemployed who could fill any job description and be glad to have the job. We live in a totally different state of affairs today in this twenty-first century.

Dad had borrowed money from his dad and bought the old place before World War II. Hog prices went up during the war, and Dad got the land paid off. After the war, people were leaving the farm life and selling their land and moving to the cities. Dad mortgaged what he owned at the time to the Federal Land Bank, and he and Mom began putting property together. I'd gotten to Texas at the end of the war (1945) and grew up as Mom and Dad struggled to make their yearly land payments for the next twenty years.

Dad bought a tract of land from Mr. Ruf Hewitt that had a large open field, and the rest of the place was grown up in cedar timber known as a cedar break. Dad cut and sold cedar fence post from time to time, and Mr. Carlowd of Roans Prairie asked Dad what he got on cedar post. Dad quoted him a price of twenty cents for a seven-foot post with a four- to five-inch top and that he, Mr. Carlowd, would pick the post up at the cedar break. Posts with eight-inch tops were cut nine feet long and were often split in half and were used to build cattle corrals. These posts usually sold for twenty-five cents each.

Dad and Mr. Carlowd haggled over the price; Mr. Carlowd was to buy one thousand fence posts at fifteen cents each, and Dad was to deliver the post. It was a big order, and one hundred fifty dollars was a lot of money. Mr. Carlowd wanted Dad to start delivering post the following week; however, Dad was busy getting some land ready to plant. So Dad hired a fellow with an ax for five dollars a day to cut post. These were good straight cedar trees that would cut two selling posts, and Dad could save the top to use in his own fences. The larger tree that would cut a nine-foot post, eight-inch top, was split in two with one selling post and the top. The man cutting the post stacked them up beside a tree so that we could see them. Dad and I would get to the cedar break about an hour before sundown and start loading the post. We'd drop the man off on our way to deliver post, stack the posts so they could be counted, and head on home to Anderson, Texas.

That first day this fellow hadn't cut but around eighty posts. Dad wasn't satisfied and told him so and that he (Dad) could cut over one hundred selling posts a day.

"If you can't cut one hundred selling posts, I'll get somebody else," Dad told the man.

The man said he hadn't swung an ax in a while but thought he could probably get a hundred tomorrow. He did cut one hundred over the next four days, but come Friday he was sitting on a post when we got there.

Dad asked, "Are you sick?"

"No, I got the one hundred posts a day cut."

I saw Dad give him that look as Dad said, "Why aren't you cutting those that you shorted me on Monday?"

The man replied, "I should have done that. If you'll pay me a nickel a post, I'll make up those twenty I was short next week, and I'll not charge for them."

Dad paid him twenty-five dollars for the five days' labor. Dad had agreed to pay him five cents a post. We picked the man up Monday morning, and that evening he had a lot more posts stacked up after we were loaded. That fourth evening when we got there to load posts, the man said he'd have all the selling posts cut by the time we got loaded. I don't think Dad believed him, but neither had Dad been checking on the man's work, for he hadn't cut any of the tops. Dad confronted the man about not cutting the tops. I could sense the contention shaping up for trouble.

The man said, "I thought you were only paying me for selling posts."

Dad stood there and then finally said, "You won't get your money until I get mine."

Years later this man asked Dad several times, "Jack, you got anything you need me to do?"

Dad's eyes looked right through him as he slightly shook his head and said, "Nope!"

THE ARTICLES

*A*nytime a cowboy draws attention to himself, he is either crazy or he's young and hasn't been fully trained in the unwritten code of the West. Or that dude is a mighty rough hand. There are many different kinds of cowboys, but only a hand is smooth as butter, and like cream, he'll just naturally rise to the top of those within a cow crowd.

This old yarn ain't hardly worth the telling of it, for it was back in my younger days when I sometimes lived on the edge. I was cowboying around a sale barn café, seeking employment among some cowboys and ranchers. I was young, and when I was given the opportunity to express my view, I said, "Most cowboys want to rope and chock everything that runs off; I like a dog that will hit, not catch, but that's fast and will hit a cow quick as she leaves that bunch."

Well, now, that raised some eyebrows. Somebody asked, "You got dogs like that?"

Now, any hand, young or old, knows not to brag on a horse, dog, or woman. If you do, you're apt to take in too much territory. So I said, "Dogs like that don't come in droves, but I've got some of the articles."

After a while, when the coffee was reheated, I was liking the mileage that I had gotten out of that bit of advertisement, so I thought I had the goods and it wouldn't hurt to advertise a little more. I hadn't learned yet that it doesn't pay to blow your own horn. I said, "There are some old, idiotic cattle that are going to run off regardless, for they have gotten away before and you ain't going to hold those cows. If the cattle ain't plum sour and I can't pen 'em, you don't have to pay me." They all thought that was fair enough; however, I didn't get one job offer.

Two weeks after I'd laid on all that talk, a fellow from over at Hempstead, Texas, called and asked if I had a pair of good dogs I'd sell and how much. I told him what I had and how much I wanted for my dogs.

I asked, "When can you come and have a look-see?"

He couldn't get away on account of his business and wanted me to come there instead. That struck me wrong, for if he really wanted to buy a dog he'd come. So I drug my feet until I was convinced he was a good prospect. Next morning I was there early at his ranch. He had several big barns, sheds, and a large cattle corral. The cattle were in this open field around this setup.

He asked, "How do you usually do this? Pen the cattle?"

I answered, "That won't be necessary, for this is open country, and you can see the dogs work." Now, I could see that wasn't the way he expected me to show him these dogs. I also noticed this was not going to be an easy place to show my stock either. All out in this field away from this setup, there were purple grass burrs boot top high.

I said, "You got a problem?" He looked at me kind of strange as I pointed at those grass burrs and said, "Very few dogs will work in those grass burrs."

"That looks like your problem, but if you can't pen these cattle, then I'm afraid we wasted each other's time."

I found myself staring, not liking the situation or the man either. I might have had a Perry look when I said, "Okay."

He said, "You've come a long ways; let me see what you got."

Today, I'd have never stayed hooked; I'd have pulled freight (left).

Back then I was young, hungry, and arrogant. I don't know why I thought I had to prove myself and dogs or show him. I dropped out a couple of dogs; as the cattle saw the dogs, they ran. My dogs were having a hard time getting to the front, let alone stopping these cattle. The cattle strung out, and this fellow knew the gig, for he took off and got ahead of most of those cattle. The front end of these cattle took out a gap (wire gate) before he got there, and he stopped the rest of the herd from following. When I rode up horseback, I could hear my dogs baying over a quarter mile away.

He said, "It's thick along that creek, and you probably won't be able to get those cattle back."

I asked, "Is that your place?"

"Yes."

I rode down and blew my dogs off the cattle with my horn. When I got back, he'd about had the gap fixed back, and I was going to mope on back to my truck and get out of that country.

He said, "Do you think you can pen those cattle with them dogs?" I knew he was talking about the two there with me and my horse.

He got another look when I said, "Maybe, maybe not! Are you interested in buying a dog or having somebody to pen your cattle?"

"I know several young men with horses that are good cowboys, but they don't have any good dogs. I'm paying two men with dogs to do the job. If you can pen these cattle with your dogs, then I will be interested in talking about buying your dogs. If you can't pen the cattle, I'm not interested in your dogs."

I said, "The grass burrs are mighty bad. Just how many dogs do these two hands use to pen these cattle?"

"They got five or six dogs."

"Do they pen all these cows every time they work 'em?"

"Not every time."

I said, "I do day work also, by the day or half day. There is only me, and I'll need the third dog that is in my trailer if I pen these cattle."

He nodded his head, so I went and got my other dog, Ol' Mitzie, that was in my trailer. It took me the better part of an hour to push those cattle up to the gate of those pens. I'd been tried several times, hard. But the old pony I was riding could operate. Those cattle didn't want to take that gate but kept going past it before the dogs had the cattle stopped. It was upon me to force the cattle to turn around and push them back toward the gate. This was where the dogs were, so I backed off the cattle until I got positioned. When I moved in, the dogs went to the opposite side of me. However, I had a blue gyp called Mitzie, the only dog I ever owned that when I said, "Load 'em," over and over, she'd help me on the back end. This time, with two dogs on the front and one in the back with me, those cattle took the pen.

This man was shutting the gate, so I asked, "You want to talk about the dogs or me finishing out a half-day working these cattle for you?"

He said the blue gyp was the only dog that really interested him and that he didn't have the medicine. Furthermore, I didn't pen them all. I shook my head, turned, and walked away. After loading my stock, I left.

I knew an old-time cowboy, Mr. Curtis Smith, that ran a boot and saddle shop in Hempstead, Texas, and as I walked into his shop, he asked, "Perry, what's eating on you?"

I smiled and said, "Your neighbor. He wouldn't pay a dime to see a jack rabbit pull a freight train."

So I had to start at the beginning and tell 'em everything. He untied his apron and pulled it over his head, grabbed his cowboy hat, and said, "Wait here, and if anyone comes in, tell them I'll be right back."

In about thirty minutes he came into the shop smiling and handed me a twenty-five-dollar check. I looked at the check and asked, "What do I owe you for collecting?"

He said, "Nothing, but be careful what you say; it can get you in a bind."

Now, that was some good advice that I've tried to live by.

THE LAST
WAKE-UP CALL

My daughter Lora Lee told me this tale about her daughter Haley. Lee said, "Dad, I thought everyone at church was acting a little unusual that morning. Most of our church family gets to church early, for we all like to greet one another. However, it dawned upon me that in our greetings, so many of the people were smiling, waving, or saying, 'We made it, Haley!' Our church recently made a new photo directory." Lee explained, "While we were all still asleep at about 5:00 a.m., it would seem Haley was up and about the Lord's business!"

Although Haley wasn't old enough to know or read her ABCs, she did know her 123s. Haley had gotten the new directory and went down the list calling everyone and asking, "Are you coming to church today?"

Lee said, "Dad, I didn't have a clue as to what was going on. Haley's in kindergarten and I didn't know she even knew how to use the phone!"

SETTING THE
BUCKET DOWN

*I*t's been my pleasure to have shared a few bygone and forgotten tales and a few fairly recent ones. But it's been a greater pleasure to share a few simple truths of the transforming powers of God. A new life begins with salvation by trusting in the completed work of the LORD Jesus Christ upon the cross. Salvation is not like vaccination. Salvation is the beginning of three parts: past, present, future. After salvation, we yield and submit our will unto the control of the Holy Spirit in lordship of life. The Spirit, and abiding in God's word, conforms us unto his image, which is our hope of glory.

To my sad surmising, the cowboy has always seemed more igno rant with a stiffer neck and a harder heart than most to ever see by faith and believe God's report. However, when a cowboy is converted, he's usually sold out to God and has become a doer of the Word and work.

It's been a pleasure. So long, ol' pard. The End.

CPSIA information can be obtained
at www.ICGtesting.com
Printed in the USA
FFOW04n1043110116
20319FF

9 781613 460924